Praise for
Ten Dumb Things Smart Christians Believe

"Ever since I read his *Unity Factor* almost twenty years ago, Larry Osborne has been my mentor from afar. Now that Larry is writing books again, he has become a go-to author for me because he speaks my language and deals with my issues. I read everything he writes!"

—PETE BRISCOE, senior pastor of Bent Tree Bible Fellowship
   and author of *Christianity: A Follower's Guide* and *Secrets from the Treadmill*

"A very liberating read, as well as one that will surely deepen your trust in God. Larry takes apart ten commonly held beliefs that don't make sense…because they aren't true!"

—RUSS CARROLL, CEO of Miva Merchant

"In *Ten Dumb Things Smart Christians Believe,* Larry Osborne dismantles many ideas that have derailed the faith of sincere Christians for far too long. Larry has the rare capacity to communicate difficult truths in a way that ignites the imagination and disarms the soul. I strongly recommend this book to anyone seeking a deeper and more-nuanced faith."

—SCOTT CHAPMAN, senior pastor of The Chapel, Illinois

"Larry Osborne never fails to compel me to think with greater precision. *Ten Dumb Things Smart Christians Believe* challenges us to reevaluate what we can so glibly believe and come away with a faith that we can deeply admire."

—DR. WAYNE CORDEIRO, author of *The Divine Mentor,*
   Doing Church as a Team, and *The Life Journal*

"I recommend anything Larry Osborne writes. He's hit another homer with *Ten Dumb Things Smart Christians Believe*! Larry unshackles our souls from things that threaten to destroy us. I'm confident your life will be better after reading this book!"

—RON FORSETH, vice president of Outreach Inc.
and general editor of SermonCentral.com

"Larry Osborne's *Ten Dumb Things Smart Christians Believe* will help new believers and seasoned Christians alike. People often believe what they've heard without knowing why. Larry pierces through widely accepted spiritual legends with common sense and scriptural precision."

—CRAIG GROESCHEL, pastor of LifeChurch.tv and author
of *Confessions of a Pastor*

"This book will liberate us from faulty assumptions about God and life that keep us trapped or looking like naive fools. Larry Osborne brings practical and biblical wisdom to bear on some beliefs that we never should've held and that have always confused us. His chapters on forgiving and judging alone are worth the price of the book."

—MEL LAWRENZ, senior pastor of Elmbrook Church
and author of *I Want to Believe*

"For a long time the world has needed this very important book. With patience and clarity, Larry dissects erroneous beliefs that masquerade as faith. He helps us wade through the nonsense—inaccurate and misguided ideas we cling to—and guides us to an understanding that results in a winsome, authentic faith…the kind we all long for."

—NANCY ORTBERG, founding partner of Teamworkx2
and author of *Looking for God*

"Larry Osborne blends pastoral experience and counterintuitive wisdom that will frustrate (in a good way), challenge, and encourage you as you seek to walk with God for a lifetime."

—DARRIN PATRICK, pastor of The Journey, St. Louis,
Missouri

"Filled with common sense from the heart, this book is a well-written and entirely biblical look at often-misunderstood principles in Scripture. I have found it not only helpful in my own life but also effective in discipling others. Great illustrations make the principles clear and easy to grasp. The game-plan illustration relating to God's will alone is worth the price of the book."

—STEVE POTRATZ, president of Parable Christian Stores and The Parable Group

"I remember exactly where I was sitting during a visit to North Coast Church when I first heard my friend Larry Osborne explode the myth that faith fixes everything. I was there to learn the inner workings of the church but walked away with new insight into my faith. Since that time Larry has taught me much about the dumb things smart Christians (and even smart pastors) believe. You'll find one 'aha' moment after another in this book. I'm buying copies for all our small-group leaders."

—NELSON SEARCY, lead pastor of The Journey Church, New York City

"Larry Osborne pulls no punches in *Ten Dumb Things Smart Christians Believe*. He brings clarity and biblical insight to commonly misunderstood ideas. With books like this one, Christians will believe fewer stupid things that damage their spiritual journeys. This book is worth reading and sharing."

—ED STETZER, coauthor of *Compelled by Love*, www.edstetzer.com

"Larry Osborne takes us through misunderstandings handed down from generation to generation, from Sunday-school class to Sunday-school class. In today's jambalaya spirituality, Larry helps spiritual seekers and misinformed churchgoers sort through the true and the ridiculous. From the barbershop to the halls of traditional church, myths are circulating…and now Larry brings the light and balance of Scripture to enlighten the misinformed."

—STACY SPENCER, senior pastor of New Direction Christian
Church, Memphis, Tennessee

"Larry's commonsense approach in addressing widely held but incorrect spiritual beliefs brings clarity and sanity—finally! The chapters on forgiveness and parenting struck a particular chord with me. Larry is a wise pastor, gifted in teaching Scripture in a way that makes biblical truth accessible and understandable. I highly recommend this book to those familiar with the Christian faith and to those who aren't."

—LINDA STANLEY, director of Next Generation Pastors
Leadership Community, Leadership Network

"I couldn't put *Ten Dumb Things Smart Christians Believe* down once I started reading it. Many Christians have the same issues Larry addresses with gentle clarity to correct thinking and behaviors. A great book for new and serious believers alike."

—DAVE TRAVIS, managing director of Leadership Network
and author of *Beyond Megachurch Myths* and *Beyond the Box:
Innovative Churches That Work*

"Smart Christians can fall for a lot of dumb beliefs. I hadn't considered how many till I read this book, chock-full of sensible observations, disarming illustrations, and compelling scriptural insights. Larry makes you laugh while he makes you think."

—KEN WERLEIN, founding pastor of Faithbridge Church,
Houston, Texas

"This is a great book. It's a life-changing message the world needs to hear. Everyone should buy a copy and read it."

—CAROLYN OSBORNE, Larry's mom

10 DUMB THINGS SMART CHRISTIANS BELIEVE

Are Urban Legends & Sunday-School Myths Damaging Your Faith?

10 DUMB THINGS SMART CHRISTIANS BELIEVE

LARRY OSBORNE

MULTNOMAH
BOOKS

TEN DUMB THINGS SMART CHRISTIANS BELIEVE
PUBLISHED BY MULTNOMAH BOOKS
12265 Oracle Boulevard, Suite 200
Colorado Springs, Colorado 80921

ISBN 978-1-60142-150-0
ISBN 978-1-60142-180-7 (electronic)

Library of Congress Cataloging-in-Publication Data
Osborne, Larry W., 1952–
    Ten dumb things smart Christians believe / Larry Osborne. — 1st ed.
        p. cm.
    Includes bibliographical references.
    ISBN 978-1-60142-150-0 — ISBN 978-1-60142-180-7 (electronic)
  1. Theology, Doctrinal—Popular works. I. Title.
    BT77.O82 2009
    230—dc22

                                        2008052742

Printed in the United States of America
2009—First Edition

10 9 8 7 6 5 4 3 2 1

SPECIAL SALES
Most WaterBrook Multnomah books are available in special quantity discounts when purchased in bulk by corporations, organizations, and special-interest groups. Custom imprinting or excerpting can also be done to fit special needs. For information, please e-mail SpecialMarkets@WaterBrookMultnomah.com or call 1-800-603-7051.

■　■　■

To Nancy, my best friend, biggest fan, most honest critic…
and the love of my life.

Contents

*verse in the Bible ■ Two conditions most people don't seem to notice ■
Are self-inflicted wounds God's doing? ■ Why Murphy matters ■ Can
a bad thing be a good thing? ■ Why we might want Jesus to wait a
while before coming back ■ The power in a path called obedience*

SPIRITUAL URBAN LEGENDS

It is no news flash that smart people can *do* some pretty dumb things. But lots of times we forget that smart people can also *believe* some pretty dumb things.

What possessed a military genius like Napoleon to think that the harsh Russian winter would be no match for his troops? Sure, they were well trained and well equipped, but it's not as if he had a shred of historical evidence to support his decision to march on.

What caused the leading scientists and thinkers of Galileo's day to ignore evidence they could see with their own eyes and brand him as a heretic and a quack?

And why would an otherwise brilliant leadership team at IBM bet the farm on mainframes and practically give away the PC, as well as the underlying operating system, to a young programmer named Bill Gates?

All of these, and many other equally baffling decisions, were made by people far smarter than you or me. Yet, in hindsight, they all look like idiots.

What happened?

In each case, an otherwise intelligent person badly misinterpreted the facts, made an incorrect assumption, or relied upon information that we now know to be completely false—with disastrous consequences. Sometimes they were confused by cultural bias (which at times can be so strong that it literally blinds us to the truth). In other cases, their underlying assumptions were so widely believed and accepted that no one thought to question them. Sometimes they were done in by a bad case of wishful thinking. But whatever the cause, they weren't alone. History is filled with examples of otherwise intelligent people who acted upon amazingly goofy assumptions—and paid a high price for doing so.

The High Price of Flawed Assumptions

We, as Christians, aren't immune. Even a highly moral, deeply sincere, smart Christian, with the best theological pedigree, has no guarantee of protection from the consequences of a bad decision based on flawed assumptions. I like to put it this way:

the wisdom of Solomon + inaccurate facts or faulty
assumptions = a fool's decision

And therein lies the reason for this book.

Over the years, I've counseled and worked with many people who have made life-altering decisions based on what they perceived to be biblical principles, only to discover too late that what they thought was biblical didn't come from the Bible at all.

Most of the time, they were victims of a spiritual urban legend. A *spiritual urban legend* is just like a secular urban legend. It's a belief, story, assumption, or truism that gets passed around as fact. In most cases the source is a friend, a Sunday-school class, a Bible study, a devotional, a book, or even a sermon.

Because they sound so plausible and come from a reputable source, spiritual urban legends are often accepted without question and then quickly passed on. Once widely disseminated, they tend to take on a life of their own. They become almost impossible to refute because "everyone" knows they're true. Anyone who dares to question their veracity gets written off as spiritually dull, lacking in faith, or liberal.

Admittedly, the consequences of some spiritual misconceptions aren't particularly devastating. For instance, if someone mistakenly believes that the Bible says that "God helps those who help themselves" or "a penny saved is a penny earned" or that Jesus was some sort of soft-skinned Western European guy with blue eyes who walked from town to town in an old bathrobe saying profound things in a wispy voice—kind of a mystical hippy on Dramamine—it will throw them off a degree or two, but it will hardly destroy their faith.

> *Spiritual urban legends aren't just harmless misunderstandings. They're spiritually dangerous errors that will eventually bring heartache and disillusionment to all who trust in them.*

But far too often the consequences are spiritually devastating. Think of the disillusionment that sets in when someone writes off God for failing to keep a promise that he never made. Or the despair that follows a step of faith that turns out to have been a leap onto thin ice.

That is why an exposé of the ten widely held but blatantly false spiritual urban legends that we're about to explore is so important. They aren't just harmless misunderstandings. They're spiritually dangerous errors that will eventually bring heartache and disillusionment to all who trust in them.

My bet is that you've already seen through a few. Others you may have always questioned, but until now thought you were the only one who didn't "buy it." Some may rock your boat. But whatever the case, I encourage you to examine each one with an open mind and an open Bible.

Measure Twice, Cut Once

There is an old carpenter's adage: "Measure twice, cut once." It's based on the observation that once we've cut a board too short, no matter how many more times we cut it, it will still be too short. The same holds true for the spiritual principles upon which we base our life. Once we've made a decision or set a course of action, it's usually too late to go back and start checking out the accuracy of our assumptions.

The Bereans of New Testament times offer an example worth following. Believers who lived in the Macedonian city of Berea, they went so far as to check out everything the apostle Paul taught them, examining the Scriptures to see if what he said was really true.

Now remember, Paul was an apostle, an author of Scripture, God's spokesman. But rather than being offended, he praised them for their lack of gullibility and noble search for the truth.[1]

I encourage you to follow their example as we work through each of the ten spiritual urban legends to come. I think you'll discover not only that they are false but also that each one flatly contradicts what the rest of the Bible teaches. In many cases, they even contradict what their so-called supporting verses, or "proof texts," actually say.

And, yes, I know that words like *dumb* and *stupid* are strong words. Whenever I use them when speaking to a larger group, I predictably get a couple of notes or even a face-to-face rebuke. Usually it's a mom trying to eradicate the words from her children's vocabulary. She wonders why I can't use kinder, gentler terms that would be more acceptable in play group.

But I can't. As noted above, these beliefs aren't just false. They aren't just unfortunate. They're not merely a few degrees off. They are dangerous. They are what the Bible calls "foolish," which in modern-day terms means "stupid" and "dumb."[2]

> *Each one of these spiritual urban legends is a bit like fool's gold. It looks great at first glance, but once tested, it proves worthless.*

Yet I want to make it clear that nothing in these pages is meant as an attack on the people who believe these things. They themselves aren't dumb. Their assumptions and beliefs are. If I'd had more room in the title, I would have called this book *Ten Dumb Things That Smart, Sincere, Good, and Godly Christians Believe.*

Each one of these spiritual urban legends is a bit like fool's gold. It looks great at first glance, but once tested, it proves worthless. No doubt we've all jumped to some pretty foolish conclusions in our lives. I know I have. But fortunately, early in my faith journey, I had some careful-thinking mentors who pointed out the folly of basing my belief system on what everybody else said rather than on careful biblical scrutiny. They taught me to avoid reading just my favorite verses. They showed me the importance of reading all the surrounding verses—and the rest of the book as well.

Their advice has served me well and saved me much heartache. It has also solidified my confidence in the Bible. The more I've learned to toss aside the clichés, happy talk, and cultural assumptions that don't fit what the Bible actually says (or the way that life really works), the greater my trust in it as God's Word and the ultimate source of spiritual truth.

It's my hope that the pages of this book will do the same for you—that they will help you question everything you hear and test everything you believe against the actual words and teaching of the Bible.

1
FAITH CAN FIX ANYTHING

I'll never forget the day my wife and I stopped by the local hospital for what we knew would be our last visit with her friend Susan.

For three years, Susan had put up a valiant fight against a disease that was now in its last stages. Her labored breathing, gaunt figure, and deep-set eyes made it painfully obvious that she would not be around much longer.

As we sat by her bed, wondering what to say and how to pray, I was stumped. (I'm a pastor and I'm supposed to know what to say in these situations.) But before I could say anything profound—or even trite—our awkward silence was broken by the entrance of Susan's husband, John, into the room.

We exchanged hugs and a quick greeting. Then John began to talk. He spoke of the plans he and Susan had for the future. Not in a regretful reflection of what could have been, but with a powerful conviction of what was yet to be.

It was weird.

Susan lay there barely cognizant, struggling for each breath, seemingly hours from death. Yet her husband stood inches away talking about future vacations, a kitchen remodel, and their retirement years as if the four of us were hanging out at a backyard barbeque.

While John and Susan had often spoken of their confidence in God's ability to heal, this was different. He wasn't talking about an assurance that she *could* be healed. He was describing his absolute certainty that she *would* be healed. He didn't have an ounce of doubt. It was already a done deal.

Then he told us what had happened. That morning, while in prayer for Susan's healing, he'd been overcome with a powerful sense of God's presence and a deep conviction that God had answered his prayer. As he continued to pray, biblical passages proclaiming God's protection and care flooded his mind. He felt as if God had physically reached down and touched him, whispering in his ear, "I've heard you. She'll be okay."

Brimming with confidence, he figured he'd arrived at the epitome of faith because he had absolute assurance of what he hoped for and complete certainty of what he had not yet seen.[1] He was as giddy as a prospector who'd just tapped into the mother lode.

I didn't know what to say. Could it be that God was up to something big? Were we about to witness a miracle? Was John's faith going to pull her back from the jaws of death?

I wasn't so sure.

He was absolutely certain.

That night she breathed her last breath.

John was devastated. For years after Susan's death, he limped along spiritually, disillusioned with God, prayer, and the impotence of faith.

But his spiritual meltdown had nothing to do with God letting him down. It had nothing to do with the promises of the Bible being hollow. It was the predictable result of having placed his trust in the fool's gold of faith's best known and most widely believed spiritual urban legend: the myth that if we have enough faith, we can do or fix anything.

Unfortunately, John's concept of faith (what it was and how it worked) didn't come from the Word of God; it came from the word on the street. He had banked on a set of assumptions and beliefs that simply weren't true. And they had let him down.

The Word on the Street

The word on the street is that faith is a potent mixture of intellectual and emotional self-control that when properly harnessed can literally change outcomes through positive thinking and clear visualization.

It's what successful people tout as the key to their achievements, survivors of great tragedies cite as the source of their endurance, televangelists credit with healing power, and motivational speakers make a sweet living espousing.

It's why, when our team is five runs down with two outs in the ninth inning, we're not supposed to think negatively. Instead, we're supposed to hang tough, visualize a big inning. Because as long as we really believe we can win, there is a good chance we will.

> *This kind of hopeful thinking is more about faith in faith than faith in God. Yet it's what many of us have been taught to believe God wants from us when we're confronted with insurmountable odds.*

Same with a medical crisis. Did the tests come back showing the cancer has metastasized? Don't panic. It can be beat. Just think positively.

Or perhaps your son is a five-foot, two-inch freshman with dreams of playing in the NBA. Whatever you do, don't discourage him. Who knows? It could happen. After all, nothing is impossible as long as he pursues his dreams with hard work and unwavering faith.

Unfortunately, this kind of hopeful thinking has nothing in common with what the Bible calls faith. It's more about faith in faith than faith in God. Yet it's what many of us have been taught to believe God wants from us when we're confronted with insurmountable odds.

We've been told that for those who can muster it up, an all-doubts-removed, count-it-as-done faith has the power to fix anything. It's God's great cure-all, a magic potion.

In fact, in some Christian circles, this kind of faith is said to have the power to actually manipulate the hand of God. I recently heard a TV preacher claim that God *has* to answer prayers of unwavering faith no matter what we ask for. As long as we have no doubt, he has no choice. It's a law of the universe. Apparently it even trumps God's sovereignty.

Though I'd hate to be the one to tell him so.

How the English Language Mucks Things Up

While faith is a concept deeply rooted in the Christian Scriptures, most of our modern ideas about it aren't. Much of the blame can be placed on the way the original manuscripts of the New Testament have been translated into English.

It's not that the translators are unskilled or deceptive. It's simply that translating anything from one language to another is a difficult task, burdened by all the ancillary meanings and uses found in one language but not another.

A quick comparison of how we use the words *faith, belief,* and *trust* in modern-day English with how they were originally used in the Greek language of the New Testament can be eye opening. Let's take a look to see what I mean.

Faith

For most of us, the word *faith* conjures up an image of confidence. It's the opposite of fear and doubt. It's often defined by our feelings as much as by anything else. That's why most teaching on faith tends to focus on eradicating all fear, doubt, and negative thoughts. It's also why "You gotta have faith" has come to mean "Think positively."

Belief

On the other hand, the word *belief* usually conjures up an image of intellectual assent. We say we believe in something as long as we think that it's probably true. And since our beliefs are thought to exist primarily between our ears, we're not particularly puzzled when people claim to believe in something—say UFOs, Bigfoot, Darwinian evolution, creationism, even Jesus—but live as if they don't. For most of us, beliefs are intellectual. Acting upon them is optional.

You can see this definition of *belief* in the way many of us approach evangelism. We tell the Jesus story to people and then ask them if they believe it. Those who say yes are immediately assured that they're headed for heaven. After all, they're "believers." It doesn't seem to matter that the Bible adds quite a few qualifiers beyond mere mental assent.[2]

Trust

In contrast to our use of *faith* and *belief,* when we use the word *trust* it almost always carries an assumption that there will be some sort of corresponding action. If we trust a person, it's supposed to show up in our response. For instance, if the parent of a teenage girl says, "I trust you," but won't let her out of the house, we'd think that parent was speaking nonsense. There's no question the daughter would.

Clearly, each of these three words carries a distinctly different meaning in the English language. But to the surprise of most Christians, almost every time we find one of these three words in our English New Testaments, each is a translation of the exact same Greek root word.[3]

That means that the Bible knows nothing of the sharp distinctions we make between faith, belief, and trust. Biblically, they not only overlap, but they are practically synonymous. To the writers of Scripture, our modern distinctions between faith, belief, and trust would seem quite strange and forced.

So, What Kind of Faith Does God Want?

The kind of faith the Bible advocates and God wants from us has far more to do with our actions than our feelings. In fact, biblical faith is so closely tied to actions of obedience that the Bible ridicules the very idea of someone claiming to have faith without acting upon it.[4]

God doesn't care if we've mastered the art of positive thinking. He's not impressed by the mental gymnastics of visualization. He doesn't even insist that we eradicate all doubts and fears. In fact, more than once, he's answered the prayers of people whose "faith" was so weak that when God said yes, they didn't believe it.[5]

When the first response to an answered prayer is shock and amazement, the people who offered that prayer certainly don't fit the standard definition of having faith. Yet God answered anyway because their prayers fit *his* definition of faith. Their simple act of praying was an act of faith—they trusted God enough to do what he commanded, even though they were certain it wouldn't work.

To better understand what biblical faith is and how it works, let's take a look at the most famous faith passage in the Bible: Hebrews 11. Often called God's Hall of Fame, it offers a lengthy list of examples, each one showing what God-pleasing faith looks like and what it produced.

The writer of Hebrews starts with Adam's son Abel, then moves on to Enoch, Noah, Abraham, Isaac, Jacob, Joseph, and Moses, laying out a series of vignettes that describe their steps of faith and the great victories that followed.

Then, almost as if he is running out of steam (or his audience is running out of attention), the writer adds twelve more examples. But this time he offers only a name or a cryptic reference to the great victories their faith accomplished.

It's an inspiring list. At first glance it seems to support the popular notion that faith rightly applied can conquer anything. It tells of kingdoms won, lions muzzled, flames quenched, weaknesses turned to strength, enemies routed, the dead raised. All in all, a pretty impressive résumé.

But the writer doesn't stop there. He goes on.

But I warn you. What he said might mess with your head. It certainly messed with mine. After reciting a litany of victories, he suddenly switches gears and changes direction. Now he speaks of people whose faith led them down a different path—folks who were tortured, jeered, flogged, imprisoned, stoned, sawed in two, and put to death by the sword. He ends with a reminder that still others were rewarded with financial destitution, persecution, and mistreatment.

Then he writes these words: "These were *all* commended for their faith, yet none of them received what had been promised."[6] In other words, these weren't the faith rejects, the losers, the ones who couldn't get it right. These were men and women whose faith was applauded by God. Yet their faith didn't fix anything.

In some cases it made matters worse.

Whoa!

I guarantee you that no one taught my kids this side of faith in Sunday school. Imagine if they did. "Okay, children, today we're going to learn how trusting and obeying God might get you torn in two, thrown into jail, hated by your friends, and force you to drive an old beater the rest of your life."

That would thin the herd.

It would certainly rile a few parents.

But it's essentially what the Bible says that faith (at least the kind of faith that God commends) might do. It may lead us to victory. It may lead us to prison. Which it will be is his call—not ours.

Why Bother?

That raises an important question. If faith is primarily about trusting God enough to do what he says, and yet it won't fix everything and sometimes will make matters worse, why bother?

One reason stands out above all others. It's what God wants

from us. He says so himself: "Without faith it is impossible to please God."[7]

Now, it seems to me that if God is really God, and not just some sort of mystical force, cosmic consultant, or favorite uncle in the sky, then knowing what he wants and doing it is a pretty important thing to pay attention to. Few of us would mess with our boss's stated preferences. What kind of fool messes with God's?

> *A thousand years from now, all the things we try so hard to fix with our positive thinking, visualization, and drive-out-all-doubt prayers won't matter. The only thing that will matter is our awesome future and our face-to-face relationship with God.*

Another reason to live by faith (even if it can't fix all the problems we face) is that it does promise to fix our biggest problem and our biggest dilemma. What do we say and do when we stand before a holy and perfect God who knows every one of our secrets and all of our sins?

Honest now—what's to keep us from becoming toast?

Frankly, nothing.

But that's where the real fix-it power of biblical faith kicks in. Jesus promised that all who believe in him (remember that includes trusting him enough to actually follow and do what he says) will receive forgiveness and the gift of eternal life.[8] A thousand years from now, all the things we try so hard to fix with our positive thinking, visualization, and drive-out-all-doubt prayers won't matter. They'll be but a distant memory, if they can be remembered at all. The only thing that will matter is our awesome future and our face-to-face relationship with God.

God's GPS System

There's one more benefit to a proper understanding of biblical faith. Biblical faith gives us something that all the positive thinking and visualization in the world can't provide. It gives us a life map, something we can depend on to always take us exactly where God wants us to go.

Admittedly, it's not always an easy map to follow. It takes time, experience, and an occasional leap into the dark to master. It can be frustrating—and scary at times. But in the end, for those who are led by it, it's a trusty guide, guaranteed to always take us where we need to be.

In many ways the adventure of learning to live by biblical faith is a lot like my love/hate relationship with the mapping software on my GPS unit. Let me explain.

I'm a geographical moron. My wife has no idea how I get home after traveling to speak somewhere. She's always surprised to see me walk through the front door.

My problem is twofold. First, I'm often in two places at once, mentally. I call it multitasking. My family and friends call it something else. But the end result is that I can be completely oblivious to my surroundings. And when that happens, I literally don't know where I am. I may think I do, but I don't, mainly because I haven't been paying attention.

My second problem is an absolute lack of an internal sense of direction. Without the Pacific Ocean and the mountains as benchmarks, I have no idea which direction is north, south, east, or west. That means that along with not knowing where I am, I often don't know where I'm heading.

Put those two together and you have a recipe for search-and-rescue. But fortunately (or so you would think), I live in a day when GPS is within reach of the common man.

Yet, despite the promise that an affordable GPS unit has to offer, there is one frustrating problem. The pesky voice in my Garmin often tells me to turn the wrong way.

My first response is always a quick flash of annoyance at the company that makes the mapping software. I wonder why they can't get it right. I know there are lots of streets they have to include, but come on. That's what I paid for. And I'm not talking about thinking I should turn left when it says to turn right. I'm talking about those times when I *know* I should turn left.

To make matters worse, as I make the turn that I know I should make, the little lady in the box starts nagging me. In a mildly disgusted tone, she repeats over and over, "Recalculating. Recalculating."

> *Faith is not a skill we master. It's not an impenetrable shield that protects us from life's hardships and trials. It's not a magic potion that removes every mess. It's a map we follow.*

It's enough to make me reach over to hit the Off button. But before I do, I'm usually struck with a haunting realization. I've been certain I was right before—but somehow ended up wrong. And despite the fact that my GPS sometimes seems unaware of a street or two and occasionally takes me on a circuitous route, it's always found a way to get me where I want to go.

But doggone it, this time I know I'm right. I'm absolutely certain. I don't care how many times she spouts off, "Recalculating." She's wrong.

So, what do I do?

This is, in essence, a crisis of faith. I have a choice to make. Will I place my trust in my own sense of direction, knowing that this time my not-so-trusty GPS has gotten it all wrong? Or will I place my faith in the little box and turn right, despite my certainty that it's directing me far from where I want to go?

You probably know the answer. Based on my past experiences, I've learned to shrug my shoulders and do what the unit says. So I reluctantly make a turn that makes no sense to me. As I do, my pulse quickens and my stomach churns. My mind fills with images of speaking engagements lost and flights missed.

I turn anyway.

And that's the reason that I always surprise my wife when I walk in the front door. Somehow east magically turns into west and the "wrong" route gets me there anyway.

Go figure.

Once I arrive at my destination, it really doesn't matter what doubts or concerns I had along the way. As long as I follow the directions or quickly get back on track after a little "recalculating," I always end up where I need to be.

That's exactly how biblical faith works. When rightly understood and applied, it doesn't matter how many doubts we have. It doesn't even matter if we're convinced that all is lost. Ultimately all that matters is whether we have enough faith (maybe just a mustard seed's worth) to follow God's instructions. Those who do, get where they're supposed to go. Those who don't, end up lost somewhere far from home.

Faith is not a skill we master. It's not an impenetrable shield that protects us from life's hardships and trials. It's not a magic potion that removes every mess. It's a map we follow.

It's designed to guide us on a path called righteousness. Along the way, it doesn't promise to fix every flat tire. It won't reroute us around every traffic jam. It won't even stop the road rage of the crazy guy we cut off at the merge.

But it will take us exactly where God wants us to go. And isn't that where we want to be?

CAN FAITH FIX ANYTHING?

They were stoned; they were sawed in two; they were put to death by the sword. They went about in sheepskins and goatskins, destitute, persecuted and mistreated—the world was not worthy of them. They wandered in deserts and mountains, and in caves and holes in the ground.

These were all commended for their faith, yet none of them received what had been promised. God had planned something better for us so that only together with us would they be made perfect.

HEBREWS 11:37–40

2 FORGIVING MEANS FORGETTING

Forgiving is not an option. It's a sacred duty, demanded by Jesus, reiterated throughout the New Testament. It's central to the Christian message.

But when it comes to actually forgiving someone of something...well, that's another matter. It's tough to do. And it's made all the harder because so many of us have never been shown what biblical forgiveness actually looks like.

Some of us have been taught that forgiveness is pretending nothing happened—a head-in-the-sand posture that ignores the obvious. Some of us think of it as a never-ending series of second chances. Others view it as a fresh start with all the consequences and old baggage removed. Still others imagine it as the immediate and full restoration of a broken relationship, complete with the same level of trust and privileges that preceded the wrongdoing.

But the goofiest idea of all is the widely held belief that genuine forgiveness means literally forgetting what happened—wiping the slate so clean that every memory of the transgression disappears.

That's what I was taught as a new Christian. I was told that if I confessed my sins to God, he would forgive them. If I confessed the same sin twice, God would be confused. He'd have no idea what I was talking about, because he'd already forgiven and forgotten the first time. Forgiveness was an act of self-induced spiritual amnesia that God did for me and I was expected to do for others.

But there was one problem with that concept. That's not how God forgives. He doesn't forget when he forgives, at least not in the sense that we commonly use the word *forget* today.

The Myth of a Forgetful God

If you look up the word *forget* in any English dictionary, you'll find its primary meaning is an inability to recall something (as in forgetting where you put the keys or forgetting to show up at an important meeting). It's the opposite of remembering.

Perhaps that's why, when the Bible says that God forgives our sins and *remembers them no more,* many of us think that means he literally erases them from memory. It's as if they never happened.[1]

Add to that other verses that speak of God removing our sins as far as the east is from the west and hurling our iniquities into the depths of the sea (with a No Fishing sign prominently placed nearby, I was told), and you can see why forgiveness has often been defined as letting go to the point of removing every trace of the wrongdoing from memory.[2]

But that's not what those verses mean or how the word *remember* is used in the Bible.

When the Bible speaks of God remembering something, it doesn't mean that a long-lost thought suddenly pops into his mind. It simply means that he renews his work with the person or situation at hand.

For instance, the Bible says that after Noah floated around for nearly five months in the ark, God remembered him.[3] That doesn't mean that Gabriel had to remind him that he'd left the hose on. It means that God renewed his work in Noah's life. From Noah's perspective, it might have seemed that God had forgotten about him. But God hadn't forgotten.

The same goes for the many biblical stories about the sins of the saints and God's subsequent forgiveness. From Adam's foolish taste test to David's mind-boggling adultery to Peter's harsh denial, the Bible tells of some pretty ugly sins. Each is prominently featured, widely known, and fully forgiven.

Now, if forgiveness means God literally has no memory of these events, we've got a bit of a theological dilemma on our hands. You and I know things God isn't aware of. The Bible contains stories he can't remember.

Obviously that's an absurdity.

So, what does the Bible mean when it speaks of God remembering our sins no more? It means that he no longer responds to us in light of those sins. They no longer derail our relationship with him. They no longer garner his wrath. They are gone—completely—from our account. But it doesn't mean he can't remember all the things we've done. An omniscient God doesn't forget stuff.

Why This Is Such a Big Deal

This is important to understand because whenever the call to forgive morphs into a call to forget, lots of us opt out. Even if we feel we *should* forgive, few of us think we *can* forgive if it means self-induced amnesia. So we don't even bother to try, except when faced with the small hurts and annoyances of life. The bigger things we hang on to.

But that's not all. When forgiving becomes synonymous with forgetting, it tends to produce spiritual confusion and other rather unfortunate spiritual responses for those of us who have been forgiven and those of us who need to forgive. Here are just a few examples.

Anger at God

When getting right with God doesn't make everything right with life, it's easy to become disillusioned and angry with God, especially if we think his forgiveness should have removed all the traces and consequences of our sin.

I've known lots of folks who have messed up big time. Many have been genuinely repentant, have turned from their sins, and have attempted to move on with their lives, only to discover that they couldn't. The chains of the past were too strong to break free.

I think of a former tax cheat who could never shake the IRS, an alcoholic dad who could never win his kids back, and a former porn addict who never regained his wife's trust or intimacy with her, no matter how hard he tried.

After a while, more than a few of these folks became angry at God. Because they assumed forgiving meant forgetting, they could not understand why God hadn't fixed everything they'd broken. They felt like he hadn't kept his part of the confession/forgiveness bargain.

Yet, in reality, God had kept his part of the bargain. He had forgiven them exactly as he promised and exactly as he had forgiven all the biblical saints of old. Unfortunately, my friends didn't know what the Scriptures actually said about forgiveness or how God worked it out in the lives of their biblical heroes. They thought they did. But they didn't.

Unreasonable Expectations

There's another problem that occurs when forgiving gets confused with forgetting. We tend to assume that if someone has forgiven us, whatever happened in the past should be a dead issue. The other person should just get over it and move on.

But that's unreasonable. It unfairly turns the tables on the one who has been wronged. It assumes his or her pain should magically disappear. And if it doesn't, we get to write off the injured party as an unforgiving slob. Our sin is now their problem. Not a bad deal!

Yet, in reality, healing takes time. Forgiveness is a decision lived out as a lengthy process. The expectation that those we've wronged should simply forget about it is not only unreasonable; it's emotionally unhealthy. People who can't remember what happened to them or who bury their pain are not spiritually mature; they're mentally or emotionally handicapped.

Giving Up

Perhaps the most significant downside of equating forgiving with forgetting is that it makes forgiveness seem impossibly out of reach.

> *Sure, we can (and should) forget the little things—the social slights, the unkind word, the idiot who jumps our parking space. But when it comes to the true hurts and injustices of life, most of us are keenly aware that self-induced spiritual amnesia isn't in the cards.*

Anyone who has been deeply hurt knows that painful memories stick. They can't be willed away. Pray as we might, they aren't erased.

The pain may lessen. The memories may fade. The nightmares may disappear. But gone for good? Not often.

Sure, we can (and should) forget the little things—the social slights, the unkind word, the idiot who jumps our parking space. But when it comes to the true hurts and injustices of life, most of us are keenly aware that self-induced spiritual amnesia isn't in the cards. It's just not possible.

And sadly, having decided that it's not possible to forget, many of us also mistakenly decide it's not possible to forgive—at least when it comes to the big stuff.

Aaron's Dilemma

I think of my friend Aaron. Confronted with an injustice that was far too big to forget and an awareness that God's call to forgive was far too important to neglect, he was caught in an emotional and spiritual quagmire.

His son had been brutally murdered by an enraged stepfather. At the trial it became obvious that the killer had a long history of abusive relationships. Two ex-wives and even his own grown children came forward to testify of terror at his hands.

After the sentencing, Aaron came to me clearly troubled. He knew he needed to move on, but he didn't see how he could ever forget—or why he would want to forget. From his perspective, letting it go completely would dishonor the memory of his son and open the door for the killer to someday walk out of jail and do it again. He had vowed to show up at any and every parole hearing to make sure that wouldn't happen. He wanted his son's murderer to stay locked up for life.

On one hand, he felt like he was honoring his son and protecting others. On the other, he feared he was damning his own soul by his inability and unwillingness to forget and move on.[4]

Fortunately, we were able to spend some time researching what the Bible actually says about forgiveness. As we did so, he realized many of his ideas about what God expected weren't rooted in Scripture. He also realized that the kind of forgiveness God wanted was not only possible, it was desirable—and it didn't mean pretending he had spiritual Alzheimer's.

How God Forgives

When it comes to forgiveness, there are two realms: the spiritual and eternal arena and the earthly and temporal arena. God's forgiveness shows up a little differently in each one.

In the spiritual and eternal realm, forgiveness wipes the slate clean. While God doesn't forget what we've done, he treats us as if it never happened. Spiritual and eternal consequences are completely removed. Judicially, our record is cleared.

But on the earthly level, things are different. God's forgiveness seldom if ever removes all the consequences or restores all that we've broken. Instead, it offers a second chance.

Let's see what I mean.

Consequences

After David's infamous tryst with Bathsheba, he eventually fessed up. He acknowledged his sin, repudiated it, and cried out to God. To his great relief, God assured him that he was forgiven and that his life would be spared.

But God's forgiveness hardly wiped the slate clean. It didn't remove the consequences. In fact, God piled on a few extra.

David was informed that the sword would never depart from his house; he'd always be at war. He was told that his own son would one day dishonor him in public as he had dishonored Bathsheba's husband in private. The temple he'd always dreamed of building for God would be left for another. And the son conceived on his night of passion would die a few days after birth.[5]

Seeing this, my friend Aaron was taken aback. He'd long known the story of David and Bathsheba. But he had never connected the dots between the kind of forgiveness God offered David and the kind of forgiveness God wanted him to offer his son's killer.

He was relieved to realize that God wasn't asking him to pretend that nothing had happened or to set aside all the earthly and legal consequences of the crime. It was perfectly appropriate for him to pursue justice and to do all that he could to make sure it was served. Forgiveness didn't mean removing all the consequences.

Second Chances

But Aaron was also challenged by the realization that along with some rather unpleasant earthly consequences, God also gave David something else that Aaron wasn't eager to give his son's killer: a second chance.

God didn't summarily doom David to a life of hopeless regret. Even though Plan A was lost forever, there was still a Plan B. It wasn't a fresh start free from all the consequences—no, they would remain with him throughout his life. But it was a genuine opportunity to become something else in the eyes of God than the murderous adulterer he had been (and technically still was).

As David returned to the path of obedience, God restored him to the highest levels of usefulness. The difficult and tragic earthly consequences continued. But at the same time, God allowed him to remain king and to actually write parts of the Bible!

Talk about second chances. God took David's best poetry and reflections (much of it written after the fiasco with Bathsheba) and published it in his holy book. And then Jesus quoted it.

That's amazing. When it comes to being restored to usefulness, making the Bible's editorial cut is as good as it gets. Who needs a *New York Times* bestseller or a Pulitzer Prize? But more important, God's dealings with David model for us a pattern of forgiveness that retains earthly consequences while offering a genuine opportunity for restoration and productivity.

Aaron realized that if his son's killer ever turned to God and sought forgiveness, he would owe him a second chance. Not a Get Out of Jail Free card or the removal of all the earthly consequences of his damnable deed, but a genuine chance to become something different in Aaron's eyes than the monster he was on that rage-filled night.

Learning to Forgive

So, how do we live out this kind of forgiveness in the real world? What consequences are appropriate? Which ones are punitive? How far do we go with second chances? Does forgiving mean trusting someone again even when we know they're untrustworthy? Does it give those who have hurt us the right to barge back into our life at deep and time-consuming levels? Do we have to invite them over for dinner…or Thanksgiving…or the wedding?

These are the tough questions. To answer them, let's see what happens when the urban legends of forgiveness are cast aside and we respond in a way that aligns more closely with what the Bible actually says about forgiveness.

Stop Keeping Score

The first thing we'll do is stop keeping score. Biblical forgiveness doesn't keep score. When Jesus spoke of forgiving seventy times (or seven times seventy, as some scholars translate the passage), he wasn't suggesting we keep a tally sheet. He was using hyperbole—or exaggeration for effect—to remind us to keep on forgiving.[6]

I think I know why. When it comes to keeping track of life's hurts, conflicts, and injustices, we all tend to use some rather creative math. We have an amazing ability to undercount our own misdeeds while multiplying the wrongdoing of others.

Think back to the last time someone nearly killed you with a dangerous lane change. My bet is that your response was pretty similar to mine. After a quick honk on the horn, a menacing stare, or a look of disgust, you were ready to move on, confident that the bozo who cut you off got the message and would be more careful next time.

But all too often, that's not how the offending party sees it. He tends to view the near accident as a no harm, no foul close call. That makes our blaring horn or evil eye a personal affront. It leaves him one down on the tit-for-tat scorecard. So he tailgates or pulls up alongside for a few choice words and some universal sign language.

We wonder, *What's with that hothead?* And if we have our own bent toward a short fuse, we're likely to do or say something to get the score back to even.

Now the battle is on. We're mere steps away from serious road rage as each party escalates the issue in the eyes of the other while simply evening the score in their own eyes.

Get a Good Mirror

Perhaps it's this tendency toward creative score keeping that prompted Jesus to give his famous parable of the unforgiving servant. It's a story about a servant who owed his king a vast amount of money. So much that it could never be repaid. When asked for an accounting, he begged his king for more time. The king gave him something better. He graciously forgave him the entire debt and sent him on his way.

You'd think that servant would be one happy former debtor. But instead he confronted another servant who owed him a small amount of money and demanded immediate payment.

When the king heard about it, he was furious. He called the servant back and—catch this—*he restored the entire debt that he had previously forgiven.* Jesus then ends the parable with these chilling words: "This is how my heavenly Father will treat each of you unless you forgive your brother from your heart."[7]

I'll leave it to the theologians to argue how literally to take Jesus's words and how far to carry the analogy of a king restoring a previously canceled debt. I can see it now: an Ultimate Fighting Championship or Cage Match between the Arminians and the Calvinists. That ought to be interesting. But in the meantime one thing is certain. When it comes to forgiveness, it's foolish to refuse to forgive others when God has already forgiven us.

That's why biblical forgiveness always starts with a look in the mirror. It doesn't start with the wrong that was done to me; it starts with the wrongs that I have done to others. It asks, "What have I done and how have I been forgiven?" And then it offers that same kind of forgiveness to others.[8]

Rebuke When Wronged, Forgive When Asked

But what happens if the person who wrongs us doesn't want to be forgiven? What happens if they keep at it? Is the Christian response to ignore it? Confront it? Teach them a lesson they won't forget?

Some say the Christian thing to do is to forgive before being asked—even as the injustice or annoyance takes place. If the school bully keeps stealing your lunch, make him an extra sandwich. If the dog next door barks all night every night, shut the windows, buy some earplugs, and turn up the TV. Same for the ex who refuses to honor your custody agreement. Forgive before they ask.

After all, didn't Jesus overlook the injustices that were done to him? Didn't he refuse to retaliate? Didn't he ask the Father to forgive those who put him to death?

Well, yes—and no.

Jesus did say of the soldiers who crucified him, "Father, forgive them, for they do not know what they are doing."[9] But that's just the point. His Roman executioners had no idea what they were doing in the cosmic scheme of things or whom they had on their hands.

But Jesus was not so quick to let the Pharisees and other religious leaders off the hook. In fact, rather than wave off their transgressions, he threatened them with hellfire. He even informed one group that a particular sin of theirs was beyond forgiveness.[10]

No question: as Christ followers, we are to forgive. But that's not the same thing as overlooking everything people say or do. Jesus did say, "Turn the other cheek." But he also said, "If your brother sins, rebuke him, and *if he repents,* forgive him."[11]

> *God's call to forgive doesn't mean we have to go through life as a punching bag. It doesn't mean we can't speak up. It doesn't mean rolling over.*

In other words, there is a time and a place for confrontation, rebuke, and pointing out our displeasure at what is being done. God's call to forgive doesn't mean we have to go through life as a punching bag. It doesn't mean we can't speak up. It doesn't mean rolling over.

Let God Be God

Ultimately, forgiveness can be given only to those who want it. For those who don't, especially those who would rather continue to hurt us than reconcile, there is another response. It's a response that many Christians aren't even aware of as an option.

It's called revenge!

To the surprise of many, there is a biblically appropriate time and place for revenge. But it's a different kind of vengeance than most of the world knows. It doesn't personally return evil for evil. For the Christian, that's not an option.[12] Instead, it turns vengeance over to God, asking him to do the honors in his perfect timing.

One day, during the trial of his son's killer, Aaron confided to me that on some nights he lay awake scheming about finding a hit man in the event the murderer was acquitted. It wasn't something he seriously considered. His thoughts were mere musings in the dark. But he felt terrible about it nonetheless. He wondered how he could be a Christian and even have such thoughts.

He was shocked when I showed him that his desires were not as out of line as he thought. There is room for revenge. But it belongs to God, not us. The problem wasn't that Aaron wanted to see his son's death avenged. The problem was that he was tempted to extract the payment himself.

The apostle Paul—the same man who wrote so eloquently about our need to forgive others—saw no inconsistency in his own prayers that God would repay his enemy Alexander for the great harm he had done. In one passage he wrote of turning Alexander over to Satan, while in another he simply said, "The Lord will repay him."[13] In still another he instructs us, "Do not take revenge, my friends, but leave room for God's wrath, for it is written: 'It is mine to avenge; I will repay,' says the Lord."[14]

In other words, sometimes it's okay to pray, "God, sic 'em!"

But if and when we do that, we still need to leave room for God's grace. He's been known to turn his (and our) enemies into his (and our) friends. And if he chooses to do so, who's to complain? That's what grace is all about. That's part of what it means to let God be God.

The Trust Issue

There is one other area of confusion that needs to be addressed. Does forgiveness mean restoring a broken relationship to its original state? Does it mean we have to trust the other person again? Does it mean we have to invite him or her to our next party?

Some people seem to think so. Once they've been forgiven, they expect to be immediately restored to full trust and relationship.

But that's not the case. Trust, close relationships, and forgiveness are not necessarily related. While forgiveness puts aside all bitterness and all plans for revenge, it doesn't make someone trustworthy or turn the person back into our best friend. Trust has to be earned. Close social ties are a privilege. We don't owe anyone either one.

I remember talking to a woman I'll call Chelsea. Her husband had been caught in an affair years earlier. Now he'd been busted again. Just like the first time, he begged for forgiveness and swore a renewed commitment to his wife and their two daughters.

She didn't believe him.

Neither did I.

But she felt guilty.

I didn't.

That's because he was never in my circle of trust. He'd proved himself to be a liar and a fraud, so based on his past history, I had no reason to believe him. No one (not even her husband) seemed to have a problem with that. He understood my hesitancy to trust him.

Yet somehow, because Chelsea had once trusted her husband (and because she confused forgiving with forgetting), she felt the pressure to immediately restore her trust in him, even though he'd proved himself to be a serial adulterer unworthy of that trust.

"I know I need to forgive him," she told me. "For the sake of our kids, I want to give him one more chance. But I don't think I can ever fully trust him again. Will God forgive me?"

I assured her that she wasn't the one in need of God's forgiveness. God wasn't asking her to trust her husband again. He was asking her to forgive him. That might or might not mean staying in the marriage. But it certainly didn't mean believing him when he called to say he was working late at the office again or claimed a flirtatious female coworker was "just a friend."

Based on his past history, that wouldn't be forgiveness. It would be credulity.[15]

How Can We Get There?

Even after we've peeled away the urban legends and myths that surround forgiveness, forgiving remains an incredibly tough thing to do. It doesn't come easy or naturally. Ultimately, it's a supernatural act motivated and empowered from the inside out.

But there are some things we can do to cooperate with God's inner prompting, to clear out the weeds of our own resistance. I've found two practices to be especially helpful.

The Prayer of Permission

We all face situations when we know what we should do but don't want to do it. The need to forgive can be one of those situations. The greater the hurt or injustice, the less I want to move toward forgiveness. It seems as though it lets the people who hurt me get away with it.

> *When we offer forgiveness to those who have no excuse—and for things most of the world would consider unforgivable—we become most like Jesus.*

That's when I turn to what I call the prayer of permission. It's a prayer I pray when I have no desire or motivation to do what I know I should do. It's a simple prayer in which I give God permission to change the way I feel about a person or situation. I don't ask him to help me forgive. I've usually asked that and gotten nowhere, because

I didn't really want to forgive in the first place. So I back up one step and give God permission to change the way I feel, to make me want to forgive.

The beauty of this prayer is that it forces me to squarely face the hardness of my heart and my subconscious resistance. I quit fighting. Once I do, the result is almost always a rapid shift in my thinking. Forgiving no longer seems like such a bad idea. And once it no longer seems like a bad idea, it's not so hard to do.[16]

A Sin Walk

The second tool that I've used to get me over the hump when I'm hesitant to forgive is what I call a sin walk. No, I don't mean a walk on the wild side. I mean a literal walk in the neighborhood or down by the beach during which I do my best to remember all my sins I can recall. And I mean *all*. I try to go back to the first brownie pilfered from Mom's cookie jar.

It's always an eye-opening exercise. It usually exposes my "righteous anger" as not being so righteous after all. It's humbling. It renews my awe and gratitude for the incredible grace and forgiveness I've received. It makes playing the role of an unforgiving servant seem ridiculous. It's also been known to send some chills down my spine and tears to my eyes.

Becoming Like Jesus

Forgiving is a big deal. It's not just for those who have done the little things that get us so worked up. It's for those who are responsible for the big stuff as well—Chelsea's unfaithful husband, the murderer of Aaron's son, and those who bring real harm and damage into our own lives.

When we offer forgiveness to those who have no excuse—and for things most of the world would consider unforgivable—we become most like Jesus. Remember, he died for sins he never committed to forgive people who had no right to be forgiven.

Maybe that's why it's such a big deal to him that we learn to forgive as we've been forgiven.

DOES FORGIVING MEAN FORGETTING?

David said to Nathan, "I have sinned against the LORD."

Nathan replied, "The LORD has taken away your sin. You are not going to die. But because by doing this you have made the enemies of the LORD show utter contempt, the son born to you will die."

2 SAMUEL 12:13–14

Bear with each other and forgive whatever grievances you may have against one another. Forgive as the Lord forgave you.

COLOSSIANS 3:13

3

A GODLY HOME GUARANTEES GODLY KIDS

Don and Sharon hate it when their Christian friends start pulling out pictures and swapping stories about kids and grandkids. They never know how to respond or what to say.

Though one of their sons is doing well—a model citizen with a great job, strong marriage, and vibrant walk with God—the other two are a mess. One is in jail. The other is pushing forty but still hasn't found himself. He's on job fifteen and marriage three. More disheartening, he's developed a disdain for spiritual things and a dependence on hard liquor. He makes no effort to stay in touch with his parents, unless, of course, he needs something, usually money.

Their two prodigals have brought Don and Sharon an abundance of heartache. It far overshadows the joy and pride their "good" son brings. It's caused them to battle with all kinds of emotions: anger, frustration, embarrassment, and shame.

But most of all, they've felt guilt—lots of guilt.

They view their two wayward sons as irrefutable proof that they failed as Christian parents. In their minds, their inability to curb the antisocial behavior of the youngest, or instill any sense of drive and moral compass in the oldest, serves as proof positive that they were lousy parents. Most of their friends agree. Not that they say so out loud. They don't have to.

In contrast, my friends Mike and Rhonda feel no guilt about their wild child. They're actually quite upbeat, confident that she will one day return to God and the values she was raised to live by.

Their confidence stems from the fact that they modeled a sincere and genuine faith. They took her to church and Sunday school each week. They gave her a solid, faith-based education. Even during her teenage years, they continued to provide strong (but not stifling) spiritual guidance to make sure she hung around the right friends, activities, and peer group. In short, they did everything they could to provide a godly, Christ-centered upbringing.

But sadly, when she went away to college things began to unravel. By the end of what should have been her senior year, she had soured on her faith, dropped out of school, and moved in with her boyfriend.

Now, years later, not much has changed. She still hasn't darkened the door of a church or tied the knot with her boyfriend. Yet Mike and Rhonda feel none of the angst or shame that Don and Sharon feel. Sure, they're disappointed. But they know that sooner or later their daughter will come to her senses and come back to God.

They're banking on God's promise that children raised the right way in a good and godly home can't stay away forever. They always come home. They can't help it. God brings them back. He promised.

Both of these couples are strong Christians. Yet their responses to their wayward children are completely different. Don and Sharon are riddled with guilt. Mike and Rhonda are filled with hope.

What gives?

Surprisingly, their vastly different emotions are both based on the same core assumption: the belief that a good and godly home guarantees good and godly kids. Don and Sharon interpret that to mean that their home was far more messed up than they had realized. Mike and Rhonda interpret it to mean that their daughter has to come back to the faith someday.

In the short run, Mike and Rhonda probably have it best. At least they have something to hope for. But in the long run, both couples are headed down a dead-end street. They've each bought into the same spiritual urban legend: the belief that a godly home guarantees godly kids. It's a lie, and every lie (even one that is widely believed and brings temporary comfort) eventually ends up being a house of cards, destined to collapse under the pressing weight of time, truth, and reality.

Where Did We Get This Idea?

Like many other spiritual urban legends, the idea that a godly home guarantees godly kids finds its source in a well-known, but widely misunderstood, Bible verse. In this case it's Proverbs 22:6: "Train a child in the way he should go, and when he is old he will not turn from it."

Most people seem to think this verse promises that a child raised *correctly* will come back to the Lord *eventually*.

But that's not what it promises—or what it says.

Proverbs Aren't Promises

To begin with, Proverbs 22:6 is not a promise. It's a proverb. Promises are absolute, especially God's. When he makes a promise, it's a done deal. You can take it to the bank. But a proverb is different. It's an observation about how life generally works. It tells us what usually happens, not what always happens.

The book of Proverbs is called Proverbs for good reason. It's comprised of God-breathed observations about life. But the observations are far from universal. The righteous aren't always honored. The wicked sometimes succeed. The diligent can lose it all, and the lazy can strike it rich.

The same goes for Solomon's encouraging words about children who are properly raised. It's a proverb, not a promise. Not many will depart from their spiritual roots. But some will.

That's why Don and Sharon's shame and guilt are so unwarranted. Their wayward offspring are no more proof that they failed as parents than the untimely death of a young Christian is proof that he or she must have been living a secret life of wickedness.

Don and Sharon may have been terrible parents. They may have been great parents. The choices and lifestyles of their grown children provide no conclusive evidence either way. Eventually their sons will have to answer to God for their own choices. In the meantime Don and Sharon will be held accountable for how they raised their children, not how their children turned out.

How Did "Won't Depart" Become "Will Come Back"?

Mike and Rhonda's confidence that their daughter will one day return to the Lord is equally unwarranted. It's not based on anything God said or promised. It's not supported by anything in the Bible. And it's certainly not based on anything found in Proverbs 22:6.

Let's look at the verse carefully and see if you don't agree.

It starts out with the phrase "Train up a child in the way he should go." At first glance, that seems pretty straightforward. But

Bible scholars disagree as to what kind of training it refers to. Some see it as a reference to training in the path of righteousness. Others claim the Hebrew phrase is better interpreted as referring to training that aligns with a child's unique personality and giftedness.

> *Most people seem to think Proverbs 22:6 promises that a child raised correctly will come back to the Lord eventually. But that's not what it promises—or what it says.*

In the long run, I'm not sure it matters. Both concepts are important and find support elsewhere in Scripture. Christian parents need to teach their children the pathway of righteousness *and* do it in a way that best fits the unique personality and gifts of the child.[1]

But it's the next phrase that gets butchered and twisted beyond recognition. Here is what it says: "And when he is old he will not turn from it."

Try as I might, I can't find anything here guaranteeing a *return* to the Lord, especially one that comes after a season of rebellion.

Can you?

How this got turned into a promise that a rebel raised in a Christian home will eventually turn back to God is beyond me. I understand why we wish it said that. But it doesn't. In fact, it says the opposite. It says they won't turn away in the first place!

The difference is immense.

Remember that this is a proverb and not a promise. So it's not saying that a properly raised child will never rebel. It's merely saying that he's unlikely to do so. In the case of those who do walk away from the Lord, this passage and the rest of the Bible are silent about their odds of returning. Even the parable of the prodigal son says nothing about the odds of a rebel returning—it just tells the story of one young man's return and his father's response.[2]

That's why Mike and Rhonda's confidence is so unfortunate. They've unintentionally given the enemy a foothold from which to attack their faith. They've set themselves up to be angry at God if their daughter never comes back, even though he never promised she would.

Why This Is Such a Devastating Myth

The myth that a godly home guarantees godly kids (and godly adults) is not just untrue. It's not just wishful thinking. It's spiritually dangerous. If we buy into it, we become especially vulnerable to two things that are never part of God's plan: unwarranted guilt and foolish pride.

Unwarranted Guilt

We've already seen how this myth can burden the parents of adult prodigals (like Don and Sharon) with guilt they don't deserve. But they aren't the only ones who get hurt. It also brings pain and boatloads of unnecessary guilt to parents whose children happen to be hyperactive, learning disabled, emotionally handicapped, strong willed, or just plain incorrigible.

You've seen it in the market or maybe in the church courtyard—a father or mother struggling with the out-of-control behavior of an unruly child.

What's the first reaction most of us have? It's usually a harsh judgment of the parents, not the child. Sure, we may say to ourselves, *What a brat!* But we also usually wonder what kind of parenting and home life produced such a little tyrant.

Tourette's syndrome, Asperger's, ADHD, or a simple case of stubbornness can make the best of homes appear to be in dire need of a visit from Child Protective Services.

One group that can get particularly hammered by this myth is adoptive parents. It's a sad scenario I've seen played out time after time.

In an incredible act of love, sacrifice, and grace, a couple reaches out to take in an unwanted or abandoned child in the hopes of not only providing a great home and a spiritual foundation, but also producing a solid citizen.

Many succeed. But for those who don't, the emotional pain and guilt can be excruciating, especially if they or their circle of friends have bought into the idea that a good and godly home *always* trumps a suspect gene pool and the foolish choices of a rebel.

Let's be honest, when the adopted son or daughter of a messed-up birth parent begins to exhibit the same academic struggles or self-destructive patterns that plagued the biological mother or father, the culprit is just as likely to be genetics as home life. For any one of us— adopted or not—there's only so much that a godly home can do to counter inherited physical or emotional inclinations.

While a misunderstanding of Proverbs 22:6 is perhaps the leading cause of unwarranted guilt among Christian parents, it's not the only culprit. So too are the lingering and subtle influences of a man named B. F. Skinner.

Skinner was an influential psychologist in the twentieth century. He believed that children are born as blank slates, able to be shaped and molded in any direction so long as we use the proper rewards and stimuli. His impact upon the social sciences, education, government policies, and modern concepts of child rearing has been enormous. Though his theories have fallen from favor over time, they still wield significant residual influence in many of our modern notions about parenting.

Ironically, many Christian leaders who would decry Skinner's atheism unwittingly advocate parenting models that mirror his theories of behavioral modification far more than they mirror anything found in the Bible.

These models are easy to recognize. They almost always come packaged as a rigid set of extrabiblical (but supposedly biblically based) rules—a one-size-fits-all recipe for parenting, education, or moral training. The rules are usually supported by a long list of Bible verses wrested out of context and accompanied by ominous warnings for anyone who dares to deviate from the prescribed pattern.

> *Every son and daughter of Adam is born with a sin nature. Sometimes it gets the upper hand. When it does, it's not someone else's fault—not even Mom or Dad's.*

But the Bible teaches something quite different from Skinner's blank-slate theory and simplistic recipes for parenting. While it implies that we have great influence and will be held responsible for *how* we raise our children, it also makes it clear that none of us can hide behind our upbringing or environment as an excuse for our wrong decisions or foolish behavior.

With God's help, we all have the capacity to overcome. That's why we're held personally responsible for our actions. When things go south, we can't cast the blame elsewhere. (Well, we can—and we do. But rumor has it that God is not particularly swayed by our excuses.)

Every son and daughter of Adam is born with a sin nature. We're saddled with a propensity for self-centered and sinful behavior. It's not something we can eliminate with a carefully controlled environment or even the prayers and godliness of a Christian parent. Our sin nature is not a mere theological concept. It's a real and present danger.

Sometimes it gets the upper hand.

When it does, it's not someone else's fault—not even Mom or Dad's.[3]

Foolish Pride

The flip side of unwarranted guilt is foolish pride. It's something I've found to be particularly prevalent among those of us who buy into the myth that good and godly homes always produce good and godly kids and just so happen to have children who are naturally compliant, easygoing, or academically gifted.

It's not hard to see why we like to take the credit. When anything turns out well, we'd all prefer to think we had something to do with it. If we've been told that good and godly kids are the result of good and godly homes, then why not pat ourselves on the back for a job well done?

I think of my friend Mitch. Raised in a horrific home, he's a testament to God's grace. Somehow he not only got saved; he also got called into ministry.

Married with two great kids, Mitch always made his family his top priority. He was determined not to make the same mistakes his abysmal parents had made. And he wanted to make sure others didn't as well. So he found a way to jam something about family values into nearly every sermon he preached. I swear he could find a family life principle in any biblical text you gave him.

He also lived what he preached. His postcard-perfect family gave him tons of credibility with his parishioners and loads of confidence in his own theories and parenting skills.

Oh yeah, one more thing. In our private conversations he tended to be pretty brutal toward our friends whose kids didn't turn out so well. He didn't understand why they couldn't do what he did and why they wouldn't follow the same step-by-step recipe he found in the Bible and the big red parenting notebook he'd picked up at a conference years before.

Then it happened—a little mistake by the lake, a vacation surprise. Suddenly, when Mitch was in his early forties, he and his wife found out that their child-rearing years were not over. A son was on his way.

At first they were thrilled. Well, kind of thrilled. Okay, shocked.

Now, seventeen years later, they're still recovering. But the shock is no longer the birth of their son; it's his total lack of responsiveness to the same methods, structures, and parenting tools that worked so well with the first two.

Mitch's son hasn't denied the faith—yet. But he's been hard to reach from the beginning. It started when he was an infant. If there was a tantrum to throw, he'd throw it. Today, if there is a line to cross, he'll cross it. I have no doubt he loves his folks and wants to please them. But for some reason he's never been able to make much sense out of their values and rules.

The jury is still out. The die is not yet cast. But at this point Mitch and his wife are clearly worried.

Looking back, Mitch can't believe how dismissive he once was of those who struggle with hard-to-control children and teenagers. He's learned the hard way the foolishness of his earlier pride. He's come to understand that the warm personalities, heart for God, and positive traits in his first two children were nowhere near as much the result of his personal handiwork as he once thought.

Needless to say, Mitch has changed his tune. The shift in the tone of his sermons is remarkable. It reminds me of the changes in my own messages over the years. I'm thankful that today my grown children are walking with God. But with the birth of each one, I came to realize with ever-increasing clarity how little I knew and how difficult the job of parenting was.

Before Nancy and I had children of our own, I would have titled a sermon on raising children something like "Ten Rules for Raising Godly Kids." But birth by birth, the titles changed. The progression went something like this:

- "Ten Rules for Raising Godly Kids"
- "Ten Guidelines for Raising Good Kids"
- "Five Principles for Raising Kids"
- "Three Suggestions for Surviving Parenthood"

If you're a parent, I'm sure you can relate. But it's not just the addition of an extra child or two (or a surprise like Mitch's youngest) that humbles the previously proud. For some of us, the foolishness of our pride doesn't get exposed until our kids become adults.

Have you noticed that many of the traits that give rise to self-congratulatory pride in the parents of naturally compliant children don't play out so well once those kids become adults? Or that many of the traits we look down on in a younger child become admirable later on in life?

The stubbornness of a three-year-old is called backbone and

conviction in a thirty-three-year-old. The highly acclaimed out-of-the-box thinking entrepreneur was most likely once a kindergartener in trouble for refusing to color between the lines. Class clowns sometimes become perpetual goof-offs, but they can also become the life of the party or the leader everyone lines up to follow. As for the can't-sit-still-for-thirty-seconds seven-year-old, he fits the early profile of the high-powered multitasking executive who just hired our compliant kid to be his office manager.

Bottom line: children aren't a mindless lump of wet clay. The products created by a potter might well reflect his skill as an artisan. But the accomplishments or sins of our children don't necessarily reflect our parenting skills or godliness any more than the output of the annual harvest necessarily represents the skill or godliness of a Christian farmer. There are way too many other variables that come into play. All we can do is our best. The final outcome is ultimately out of our hands.[4]

A Lesson from the Garden of Eden

The Bible contains a story that should once and for all cut the legs out from under the myth of a godly environment guaranteeing godly kids. But I'm afraid that we often miss it. Yet it's one of the most important lessons to be learned from the Garden of Eden.

It doesn't get much better than a perfect environment, perfect parenting (if we can call God's instructions to Adam and Eve parenting), and the complete absence of a sin nature. Yet we all know what happened. Things didn't go so well. Adam and Eve disobeyed, and we're all still caught in the backwash of their rebellion.[5]

If nothing else, the fall of Adam and Eve should put to bed the idea that environment controls outcomes. If rebellion happened there, it can happen anywhere, even in the best of Christian homes.

Whatever Happened to Bad?

I'm also afraid that somehow we've lost sight of the simple truth that some people (and some children) are incorrigible. Have you noticed that there no longer seems to be such a thing as a "bad" kid? There are only victims: children whose behavior is the fault of a poor education, a lack of opportunity, poverty, an emotional handicap, a dysfunctional family, or something—anything—but them.

It's as if a terrible report card with poor grades and worse citizenship no longer elicits a rebuke of the child. Now these things raise a question about the parents. Which is it—the gene pool or family environment?

Everything is someone else's fault.

Parenting Still Matters

None of this is meant to say that parents don't have responsibility for how they raise their children. Or that it doesn't matter how we parent. It does.

The Old Testament places a high priority on godly parenting. One story sums up how important it is. A highly honored high priest by the name of Eli sloughed off his responsibility and made no attempt to restrain the sins of his two sons. As a result, God not only struck his sons dead, but he also took away the life and legacy of Eli. And he made sure it was all faithfully recorded as warning to us all.[6]

The New Testament also makes it clear that passing the spiritual torch should be a top concern for every Christian parent. Nothing says that more than the requirement that those who offer leadership in the church must first have their household in order and also have children who are believers.[7]

That seems to clearly imply that in God's eyes, our home life is more important than any other ministry we might have. Parenting, and parenting well, is a top spiritual priority.

But at the same time, notice that not allowing those whose children aren't believers to lead is not an indictment on those of us with struggles at home. It's simply a statement that if things aren't right with our children, we need to concentrate on getting our family in order before tackling the difficult task of leading God's family. To read the scriptural prohibition against a parent with a godless child taking on public leadership as an indictment on the parent would logically mean that the next verse prohibiting putting new believers into a position of leadership is an indictment against new Christians—an obvious absurdity.[8]

Parenting is a tough job. Advice is easy. So is critique. But for those of us in the midst of the battle, it's not so simple. Things that sound easy in a seminar or Bible study are usually a lot more nuanced in real life.

> *Parenting is a tough job. Advice is easy. So is critique. But for those of us in the midst of the battle, it's not so simple.*

I'm reminded of the simple advice to keep my cool and never discipline my children in anger. Sounds good. Makes sense. But I, for one, could never figure out how to pull it off. What was I supposed to do? Wait until we were all having a good time—then *bam!*?

Rather than preening in pride, casting harsh judgments, or wallowing in self-pity and unwarranted guilt, we simply need to cast aside the myth that produces these unsavory responses and live in light of the truth. As parents, we do have a sacred responsibility for how we raise our kids. But we have no ultimate control over how they turn out.

Admittedly, there are plenty of Christian parents who have good reason to feel guilty. Hypocrisy, angry outbursts, inattention (or its mirror opposite, hyper control), poor marriages, and broken homes are all too common. The price for each is always high.

But when godly parents do the best they can and yet fail to achieve the outcome they hope for, they need a break, not a drive-by "guilting." And when things go well, we need a lot more gratitude and a lot less pride.[9]

So, if you're a parent, give it your best shot—then go take a nap. And if you've already given it your best shot—take a long nap. You deserve it.

DOES A GODLY HOME GUARANTEE GODLY KIDS?

Train a child in the way he should go, and when he is old he will not turn from it.

PROVERBS 22:6

The soul who sins is the one who will die. *The son will not share the guilt of the father, nor will the father share the guilt of the son.* The righteousness of the righteous man will be credited to him, and the wickedness of the wicked will be charged against him.

EZEKIEL 18:20

4
GOD HAS A BLUEPRINT FOR MY LIFE

Have you noticed that when it comes time to make a major decision, most of us experience a heightened interest in discovering God's will? Not that we don't care the rest of the time. But when making a choice about a job opportunity, selecting a college, determining the future of a romantic relationship, or deciding where to live, we don't want to blow it. So we seek God's will with extra fervor. We pray for it, ask about it, search for it. All in the hopes that it will become clear what God wants us to do.

Some of us look for signs, divine coincidences, and open doors that supposedly indicate God's leading. Others look deep within, seeking a supernatural insight or a sense of inner peace to show the way. Still others play Bible roulette, flipping through pages of the Bible until they find a passage that seems to speak directly to their situation. Some of us major on fact finding and wise counsel or at least the advice of a few friends. Almost all of us pray a little more: *Lord, show me your will—please.*

As I've watched the way we go about trying to determine God's will, I've become convinced that the majority of us assume that God's will is both important AND elusive.

It's *important* for obvious reasons. Any time God has a specific plan or a preference in mind, only a fool ignores it. A bigger fool defies it. Just ask Jonah.[1] He found out that defiance is not a good option. So have I. My bet is that you have too.

As for God's will being *elusive,* it's elusive because…well…it just is.

Isn't it?

Which raises a troubling question: if God's will is so important, why is it so hard to find?

The surprising answer is that it isn't hard to find. Most of God's will is spelled out in black and white. It's not hidden. There's no cosmic Easter egg hunt required to see who can find it and who gets left with an empty basket.

But unfortunately, that's how many of us feel. For some of us, no matter how hard we search, we keep coming back with an empty basket.

> *There's no cosmic Easter egg hunt required to see who can find God's will and who gets left with an empty basket. But unfortunately, that's how many of us feel.*

Here's why. In many cases we're looking for the wrong thing. We're like a young child who mistakenly thinks that Easter eggs are square and polka dotted, so we walk right past the one thing we want most in search of something we'll never find.

The problem stems from a concept many of us have been taught from birth. We've been led to believe that God has a highly detailed blueprint for our life that includes a specific, preordained job, career, house, spouse, car—and everything in between.

As a result, we spend a lot of time looking for that special person, place, or thing that we think God has set aside just for us. It's the egg we hunt for.

But that egg doesn't exist. The idea of a detailed blueprint for our life is a myth. It confuses God's omniscience with his divine will. No question, God knows everything, down to the number of hairs on our head. But that doesn't mean he has a plan for how many we have or that we're in rebellion if we try to replace some of the ones that go missing.

The fact is, God doesn't have a blueprint for our life. Never has. Never will. He does, however, have a game plan for our life. And the difference is important.

Blueprints

Consider how a blueprint works. A blueprint contains a specific set of instructions that spell out everything in detail. It's so specific that anyone with the ability to read and follow a set of plans can build exactly what the architect had in mind.

But imagine a builder who doesn't agree with the architect's design and ignores the parts of the blueprint he doesn't like or understand. He'll soon have a major problem on his hands. Along with suffering the wrath of the architect, he'll also have to face the ire of a building inspector. Even worse, he'll eventually have to pay the cost of restoring everything back to what the plans originally called for.

You don't mess with blueprints. You follow them.

For many of us, this is our metaphor of God's will.

Game Plans

A game plan is very different. Rather than spelling out everything in detail, it sets forth general guidelines and principles, with lots of freedom and flexibility for adjustments as the game unfolds.

Let's take a football game as an example. On-the-fly adjustments are built into every play. What starts out as a post pattern turns into something else altogether if the linebackers blitz or the receivers aren't open. No quarterback throws the ball to a well-covered receiver just because that's the way the play was originally designed (unless he wants to sit on the bench or his name is Brett Favre). Instead he tucks the ball away and heads for the sidelines or up the field.

Now, that doesn't mean it's a case of "Do as you please." The quarterback can't decide to run out of bounds and then sneak back onto the field. He can't throw a pass to an ineligible receiver. Those moves aren't allowed. But within the rules of the game, he has lots of options. If Plan A breaks down, he's expected to try something else to help win the game.

Not so with a blueprint. It has no Plan B. If Plan A gets messed up, everything is messed up. It's back to the drawing board.

Are You Sure You Want a Blueprint?

I find that lots of people are discomforted at the thought that God might not have a detailed blueprint for every aspect of their life. That idea has been so ingrained in them that it's become a source of great comfort and reassurance. But think about it for a moment. Do you really want a detailed blueprint for your life?

Imagine what would happen if God's will for our life was actually like a blueprint, detailed down to the parking space he has set aside for us during the holiday rush at the shopping mall.

What happens when, in a fallen world, others decide to ignore God's blueprints for their lives? It's not so bad if they take our parking space. But what if they buy the house God had picked out for us? Or cheat on an entrance exam and take the last open spot in the college we were supposed to go to?

Oh no, you say. That can't happen. God knows everything and would step in and stop it.

Really? If so, isn't humankind's free will just a sham?

Or what happens if, in a moment of spiritual rebellion, Joe Christian dates and marries the wrong woman? If God won't allow that to happen, then we're not much more than puppets on a string. If he does allow it, Joe might have just put the whole world in a jam.

Here's what I mean. The poor girl he was supposed to marry is stuck, her blueprint ruined forever. Same for the guy who was originally intended to marry Joe's new wife. Unless those two both stay single or marry one another, Joe may well have started a chain reaction that will eventually mess up marriages worldwide—which just might explain a lot of things.

This is not to say that God *never* has a specific and highly detailed plan in mind. Sometimes he does. He told Hosea to marry Gomer. He told Moses and the children of Israel exactly where to camp and when to move during their wanderings in the wilderness. He sent Jeremiah to a potter's house and told him to watch for an object lesson. He changed the apostle Paul's itinerary and would not allow him to go into Asia or Bithynia.[2] But these kinds of explicit instructions are exceptions, not the norm—even in the lives of our biblical heroes.

The fact is, we have much greater freedom than any blueprint would allow. That's the main reason the details of God's will sometimes seem hard to find. They often aren't there. We're asking God, "Which one?" And he's saying, "I don't care. It's up to you."

In the vast majority of situations and decisions, we have great latitude. God doesn't care where we work so much as how we work, where we live so much as how we live, and even whom we marry (as long as it's within the faith) so much as how we do marriage.

Just look at the actual words of the New Testament. You'll notice there is little emphasis on the kinds of decisions we commonly stress over. Instead, the primary emphasis is on godly character and daily obedience as our pattern of life.

> *God doesn't care where we work so much as how we work, where we live so much as how we live, and even whom we marry (as long as it's within the faith) so much as how we do marriage.*

Certainly, when faced with a decision, we should pause to check the Scriptures and ask God if he has any specific input. If he does (either through the Scriptures or the inner leading of the Spirit), we must do exactly as he says or leads. But we shouldn't be surprised when most of the time his silence says, "I don't care—this one is your call."

More Downsides

But that's not all. A blueprint mentality has other significant spiritual downsides. Besides being an inaccurate and faulty metaphor for how God's will actually works, it also tends to produce a couple of dangerous spiritual side effects, in particular paralyzing fear and a skewed focus. Here's why and how.

Paralyzed by Fear

One of my sons currently works as an estimator for a commercial painting company. His job is to take a set of blueprints (often a couple of inches thick) and pull out everything that has to do with painting the project. He notes the square footage, the walls, trim, ceilings, and scheduled time lines. He also has to catch any side notes that call for a specific finish or materials. Based on what he comes up with, the company decides a price and bids the job.

A subcontractor's worst nightmare (and thus my son's nightmare) is to miss something significant on the plans and to submit a bid low enough to get the job but too low to finish the job profitably once the overlooked specs are added back in. It's what keeps a novice lying awake at night.

I've noticed that lots of Christians with a blueprint mentality approach every major decision like a rookie estimator approaches a set of plans. They're petrified of making a mistake.

A friend of mine could never pull the trigger to get married. In the absence of a "clear yes" from God (I'm still not sure what a "clear yes" was supposed to look like), he was afraid to move forward. He was so fearful of marrying the "wrong one" that he now looks back regretfully at all the good ones who got away.

But that's what a blueprint mentality does. In the mistaken belief that there is only one right choice for every major area of life, it paralyzes decision making. As a result, we can end up hesitating, overthinking, and rejecting lots of good and acceptable options.

This is why I like to tell my friends who get their shorts wadded up over every major decision to relax. If the Scriptures tell us what to do, then by all means let's do it—and do it right now. But if not, let's make the best choice we can and move on. After dying for our sins and paving the way for our adoption into his family, God won't doom us to a life of regret because we picked the "wrong" college, major, job, or even spouse. And even if we do make a mistake, there is always a path of obedience in every situation—even on the back end of some really stupid decisions. I know. I've been there. It works out okay.

Skewed Focus

Another problem with a blueprint mentality is that it tends to turn our focus toward the wrong things. Instead of worrying about the weightier matters of godliness—justice, mercy, and obedience—we fixate on finding the right mate, choosing the right career, or renting the right apartment.

I'm not saying these decisions are unimportant. They are. Decisions ultimately create destiny. But they aren't nearly as important as a life of daily obedience.

For instance, I'm amazed how often people ask me for prayer regarding whether it's God's will for them to marry someone they're dating—all the while blatantly ignoring his will for their sexuality. I'm never quite sure how to respond. They ask with such sincerity. It's as if it has never dawned on them that God might not bother to show them *whom* to marry when they're already ignoring his instructions about *how* to date.

It's not as if God's will for their sexuality is hard to find. It's clearly spelled out in the Bible.[3] In most cases they already know what he wants. They just don't think it works for them at the moment.

Their great error is the mistaken assumption that choosing the right mate will trump living the wrong life. As a result, they treat God as a part-time blueprint consultant—someone to turn to for the really big decisions, but someone who's not particularly relevant on the day-to-day stuff.

But that's a problem.

God doesn't do consulting.

He does God.

It's obviously unfair to paint with such a broad brush as to imply that everyone who sees God's will as a detailed blueprint ignores God's day-to-day commands. That's clearly not the case. But a blueprint mind-set does tend to turn our focus more toward *finding* rather than *becoming*.

I remember asking a college group I was leading to list all the traits they were looking for in an ideal mate. The lists were impressive. They revealed what most of the students were looking for: mates perfectly suited just for them.

Then I asked everyone to look at their list again. This time, instead of focusing on what they were looking for and where they might find such a person, I suggested they ask another question. "Why would a person like this want to marry *you*?"

The room became strangely quiet.

Their blueprint mentality had put them in search mode. Most of them hadn't even considered that God's will for their future marriage might involve more than finding the right mate or that the most important key to a great marriage might be who they would become, not who they would find.

Understanding God's Game Plan

Besides being a far more accurate metaphor for how God's will works, seeing God's will as a game plan emphasizes that the knowledge of

God's will is easily within reach. All of the basic guidelines and principles are found in Scripture. With the basics in hand, we can know what to do, what not to do, how to think, and how to live no matter how unusual the situation or complex the decision may be.

Yet while mastering God's game plan is pretty simple on the one hand, it's also highly nuanced on the other. The longer we're at it, the deeper and better our understanding becomes. But it's not out of reach for even the newest of Christians. Jesus put it this way: "Come to me, all you who are weary and burdened, and I will give you rest. Take my yoke [a steering guide] upon you and learn from me, for I am gentle and humble in heart, and you will find rest for your souls. *For my yoke is easy and my burden is light.*"[4] So with that in mind, let's take a brief flyby of the basics of God's will—the things that, once mastered, will turn the process of finding and being in God's will into a journey to become someone rather than a search to find something elusive.

Obey What We Know

The starting place for finding God's will is obeying the commands and instructions we already know. The pathway of obedience always leads to further light. It's what I like to call the dimmer switch principle. If we obey the light we have, we get more. If we disobey the light we have, we get less.[5]

That helps to explain why it's such a waste of time to seek God's leading for a major crossroads decision if we are currently disobeying him in the things we already know. We can pray all we want. But if we're in the midst of high-handed disobedience, God won't answer.

In fact, he actually calls such prayers detestable. He even says he'll laugh at our predicament rather than help. Now, I know that sounds very un-Godlike. But you'll have to take it up with him. Because that's exactly what he says he'll do.[6]

That's why I like to tell new Christians not to worry about all the things they don't know. The same goes for the rest of us. If we simply start with what we already know and then do it, the rest always comes in time.

Get the Facts—As Many As Possible

To follow any game plan, especially God's game plan, we have to use our brain. The facts always matter, even in the spiritual realm. Long ago, Solomon noted that the wise and righteous check the facts before choosing a course of action, whereas fools don't bother, jump to conclusions, or ignore the facts altogether.[7] Unfortunately, in some circles, questioning a spiritual leader, rigorously checking the facts, or hesitating before we jump is labeled as unspiritual, as if faith and facts are somehow incompatible. Nothing could be further from the truth. Even the apostle Paul praised those who carefully checked out what he said and made him prove his points with Scripture.[8]

Biblical faith is not illogical. It doesn't deny or ignore the facts. It fits the facts. Certainly we might not always understand what God is up to or how doing things his way can possibly work out in a particular situation. But I would suggest that it is never illogical to do what God *clearly* tells us to do. It's the most logical thing in the world.

The real issue we all face is determining if our latest crazy idea is really from God or not. In other words, was that dream from the Lord or last night's pizza? The only way to know is to put it to the test, and that demands a hard look at the facts. It's the only way to know with certainty the difference between a harebrained idea and the legitimate leading of the Lord.[9]

To see what I mean, let's look at one of the most extreme faith stories in the Bible: the story of Abraham's willingness to sacrifice his son Isaac.

If you know the story, you know that when God asked Abraham to sacrifice Isaac, they both immediately headed to the mountain to do so, seemingly with no questions asked. At the last moment God stepped in and said, "Just testing." He provided a ram caught in a bush as a substitute for Isaac and affirmed Abraham's faith.[10]

At first glance, Abraham's actions defy logic. Most of us (okay, all of us) think, *I'd never do that.* But a careful look at the back story puts things in a different light. Abraham's actions weren't illogical. They fit the facts. He used his brain. In fact, the facts surrounding the situation are what gave him such confidence that God was behind the bizarre request and would work everything out.[11]

Don't forget that for decades God had spoken to Abraham face to face. During that time, he'd made a series of increasingly difficult-to-fulfill promises and each time came through, culminating with the birth of Isaac long after Abraham and his wife were physically able to pull it off. Isaac was the ultimate "miracle baby." Well, outside of Jesus, that is.

Based on these past experiences and the hard facts of the situation, Abraham would have been a fool to disobey. There was no doubt it was God himself delivering the command. The instructions weren't cryptic. And God had already shown himself to be completely faithful to his promises.

We aren't all that different. If God has a huge, Abraham-like step of faith he wants us to take, there will be no doubt about what he wants us to do and the facts will bear it out. But like Abraham, before doing something rash, we first need to be sure we have the facts straight and use our brain to confirm that this is really what God wants us to do.

Using our brain is a big part of following any game plan, especially God's. He gave it to us for a reason. It's always a good idea to use it.

Think Biblically

It's hard for an athlete to follow a game plan if he misses all the team meetings. It's just as hard to follow God's game plan if we don't know the Scriptures (what they actually say, as opposed to what we might think they say).[12]

Yet the current state of biblical illiteracy among self-described Christians is far from encouraging. I remember when WWJD? (What Would Jesus Do?) bracelets were all the rage. I found that many folks who wore one had no idea what Jesus actually said or did—or even how to look it up.

Occasionally (the devil made me do it) I'd ask someone wearing one of the bracelets if they could help me remember the Ten Commandments, find the Sermon on the Mount, or locate the passage where Jesus said, "Love your neighbor as yourself." Most couldn't. Though a few were pretty sure they'd seen the verse about early to bed and early to rise making one healthy, wealthy, and wise.

It does us no good to try and do what Jesus would do if we have no idea what Jesus actually did. It's not enough to make our best guess. God's game plan is way too counterintuitive for that. None of us is likely to come up with loving our enemies, serving those we lead, or keeping our word at all costs. Those kinds of responses only come from spending time with the playbook.

Master the Basics

In sports, they're called the fundamentals—the basic skills needed to play the game. Whether it's tennis, golf, or football, there are some skills every player has to master in order to have a chance to win.

The same holds true for God's will: there are some fundamental parts of his game plan that we have to master in order to experience it. These fundamentals are made up of the clear, black-and-white commands of Scripture. They tell us explicitly what God wants us to do or not do in any situation—things like tell the truth, be kind, and always repay good for evil. No matter how deep the weeds or how difficult a decision or dilemma may be, the fundamentals can be counted on to steer us in the right direction.

The most basic of all are the passages that go so far as to specifically state, "This is what God wants" or "This is God's will." They are a great place to start.

For instance, we're told that God wants everyone to come to the point of repentance (a spiritual turnaround that results in following Jesus).[13] So it's probably not worth asking him to show us his will for a major decision if we're not willing to follow his Son on a daily basis.

> *Our job is not so much to find something; it's to become someone—a reflection of his image and character no matter where we find ourselves.*

The Scriptures also tell us that it's God's will that every Christian be filled (controlled by) the Holy Spirit, that he wants us to be sexually pure and to avoid all forms of immorality, and that it's his will for us to respond with respect and obedience to the authorities in our life.[14]

When I look at that list—and actually read the verses—I can't help being convicted by how many times I (and many other Christians I've known) have sought God's specific leading for some esoteric decision while ignoring the fundamentals of his game plan. Once again, it really makes no sense to ask God if I should apply for a promotion when I'm failing to show respect to my current boss, to ask what college he wants me to go to when I'm messing around with my girlfriend, to seek his direction and help when I resist the words of the Spirit in Scripture or the whisper of the Spirit in my heart.

God, indeed, does have a plan for all of us. But it's a game plan with lots of freedom, not a blueprint with every detail spelled out. Our job is not so much to find something; it's to become someone— a reflection of his image and character no matter where we find ourselves.

DOES GOD HAVE A BLUEPRINT FOR MY LIFE?

Do not conform any longer to the pattern of this world, but be transformed by the renewing of your mind. *Then you will be able to test and approve what God's will is—his good, pleasing and perfect will.*

ROMANS 12:2

Do not be foolish, but *understand what the Lord's will is.* Do not get drunk on wine, which leads to debauchery. Instead, *be filled with the Spirit.*

EPHESIANS 5:17–18

5 CHRISTIANS SHOULDN'T JUDGE

I have a surefire way to get your non-Christian friends or coworkers to quote the Bible. It works every time.

Use the *s* word.

Call something a sin.

Speak out against a lifestyle the Bible forbids. Critique the belief system of a cult or world religion. Or criticize any behavior that isn't universally condemned by our culture. Then step back and wait.

It won't be long until someone who otherwise doesn't have much use for the Bible quotes from Matthew 7:1. "Judge not" (NKJV).

Ironically, the person who speaks up will probably have no idea where to find the quoted verse—and no idea that it's quoted out of context.

The Judging Myth

The idea that Jesus forbade his followers to judge is a myth. It's another widely believed spiritual urban legend that can't stand up to the actual words of Scripture. Refusing to make judgments or call sin, sin, is not what Jesus asks us to do. As we'll see, he did so all the time. And he asks us to do the same. Refusing to do so leads to costly spiritual consequences, not only in the lives of those of us who refuse to judge, but also in the lives of those who never have their sins pointed out.

> *Refusing to make judgments or call sin, sin, is not what Jesus asks us to do. He did so all the time. And he asks us to do the same.*

Jesus didn't say, "Judge not," followed by a period—or an exclamation point. He said, "Do not judge," followed by a clarification of what type of judgments to make, when to make them, and how to make them. The Matthew 7 passage, read in context, isn't a prohibition against judging. It's a stern warning against judging improperly. In fact, immediately after saying "Judge not," Jesus goes on to tell us not to give our sacred things to dogs or to cast our pearls before swine.[1] That's hard to do without making a few judgments, especially in regard to figuring out who is a "dog" and who is a "swine." The same goes for verses further on in that chapter, where Jesus implores us to carefully inspect the spiritual fruit of anyone who claims to speak for God, rejecting those who bear bad fruit and listening to those who bear good fruit.[2]

So, why do so many of us think that Jesus doesn't want us to judge?

There are a couple of reasons. One, as we've just seen, is a failure to read the rest of the passage and interpret Jesus's words in context. The other is our natural tendency to interpret ancient words through the filter of our modern-day culture, especially a highly valued trait we call tolerance.

The Tolerance Filter

Today, *tolerance* is mostly defined as allowing others to believe and live in ways that we don't agree with, supporting their right to do so, and refusing to judge their viewpoint and actions as being either right or wrong. As a result, in most circles, criticizing someone else's beliefs or moral choices is considered to be a major social faux pas, a sure sign of arrogance or ignorance.

And for those who know that even Jesus said, "Judge not," that seals the deal. That moves judging others from being merely politically incorrect to flat-out wrong.

Except for one problem: that's not what Jesus actually said. And it's certainly not what he meant. He not only told his followers to judge, he also gave them instructions for how to judge properly. And he did quite a bit of judging himself.

Tolerance Redefined

This is not to say that an emphasis on tolerance is a bad thing. Rightly understood, it's a great thing—a necessary part of the social fabric for any diverse society. It's also a trait that every Christ follower should strive for.

But unfortunately *tolerance* no longer means what it used to mean. It once meant granting others the freedom to be wrong. It didn't preclude critique and criticism; it simply sought to offer evaluation in a spirit of grace and humility. That's a long way from today's definition of *tolerance* as affirming that everyone is right, no matter what they believe or what they do.

This new definition of *tolerance* has become so widely adopted that even many Christians believe that it's inappropriate to critique or criticize the religious beliefs or moral standards of others.

In many ways, that's understandable, because it's never easy to get outside of the values and viewpoints of our day. If you doubt me, just look back at what you thought was cool and hip fifteen years ago. Or take a peek at the pictures in any high school yearbook. You'll find a silent testimony to our herd instinct.

Yet if we follow the crowd on this one and buy into the belief that we should never judge others, we'll end up going down a trail that not only differs from what Jesus said but also defies logic, obscures truth, and propagates sin.

The Truth About Spiritual Truth

Underlying the idea that we have no right to judge the beliefs and moral standards of others is another widely held belief. It's the dogma that truth and morality are relative—the conviction that there are no universal spiritual truths and no universal moral standards. In other words, in the spiritual and moral realms, two diametrically opposing viewpoints or standards can both be true at the same time.

Yet this is an idea that is accepted nowhere else. Only in the moral and spiritual realm do we buy such nonsense.

Imagine an engineering student arguing that his calculations don't matter as long as they work for him. Not many of us would drive over a bridge he designed. Or imagine your doctor giving you a handful of pills and telling you to take whichever ones "feel right."

In every area of life where we can test outcomes, we know that some things work and some don't. Some answers are correct and some aren't. The belief that the spiritual and moral realms operate differently is an unsupported leap in logic. It's a dark journey into an *Alice in Wonderland* world where fanciful and wishful thinking replaces reality and common sense.

Why We Need to Judge

Jesus and the Bible not only don't forbid judging, they actually give us a set of principles and lenses through which to judge.[3]

Think about it: if we were forbidden to make moral and spiritual judgments, we would have no objective way to distinguish between truth and error. But Jesus told us how to judge precisely because some beliefs are true and some are false, because some actions are right and some are wrong.

Not long ago I heard a political pundit refer to the story of Jesus and the woman caught in adultery.[4] In an attempt to defend the questionable behavior of his favorite candidate, he pointed out that when the religious leaders brought the woman to Jesus, he stopped them in their tracks by insisting that the person without sin cast the first stone—and then after all her accusers had left, he said to her, "Neither do I condemn you."[5]

> *If we were forbidden to make moral and spiritual judgments, we would have no objective way to distinguish between truth and error.*

"I stand in the tradition of Jesus," the pundit proclaimed. "I don't judge people."

One problem, though. Jesus did judge people. To the woman in question, he didn't only say, "Neither do I condemn you." He also went on to say, "Go now and leave your life of sin." That's a judgment. He didn't ignore her adultery. He didn't wink at it. He didn't say, "I'm personally uncomfortable with it, but as long as it works for you, that's okay." He called it what it was—sin. No question, he confronted her with grace. But he also confronted her with truth and warned her to make some serious changes—soon.

If we refuse to label the behaviors Jesus called sin, sin, we're disagreeing with Jesus, not following Jesus.

The proper course of action is not to stop judging others; it's to judge properly, in line with the standards and principles of judgment that Jesus taught. At the same time, it's no news flash that some of us who understand that it's okay to judge go about it in ways that do more harm than good. So let's look at what Jesus and Scripture actually say about this thing called judging and what it takes to get it right.

Judge as We Want to Be Judged

One of the first keys to judging appropriately is to remember that the standard we use to judge others will be the standard God uses to judge us.[6]

That doesn't mean that if we overlook or ignore the sins of others we can sin with impunity (which often seems to be an underlying assumption of those who don't want to judge anyone or anything). It does mean we need to judge with extreme caution and clarity.

Beware of "Balancing the Scales"

This warning is particularly significant for those of us in positions of moral authority, such as teachers, preachers, and parents. I know firsthand how easy it is to condemn the very things we struggle with most. In fact, I think it's these things that we're prone to judge most harshly.

I've often wondered why. On the surface, it makes no sense. It seems like the hypocrisy would be hard to live with. But it's obviously not. Too many of us do it.

Perhaps it's an attempt to balance the scales (crusading against the sins we struggle with, as if loudly condemning something makes up for secretly doing it). Or maybe it's an effort to convince God and ourselves that we're still on his side despite the evil we just can't seem to beat.

You probably remember the sad story of Jimmy Swaggart, the southern hellfire-and-brimstone preacher who gained a huge television following during the 1980s. He had a particular disdain for the evils of sex. With fiery passion, he preached against anything or anyone he saw as a purveyor of temptation.

After he was busted for a series of voyeuristic meetings with a local prostitute, it all became clear. He hadn't been preaching to his congregation. He'd been preaching to himself. But sadly, according to the words of Jesus, he had also been condemning himself with every sermon he gave.[7]

Beware of Overprotection

Another reason we sometimes harshly condemn the sins we struggle with is our desire to protect those we love. We don't want them to endure the same pain and heartache we've gone through, so we step up the rhetoric and rail against the sins that cause us the most trouble.

I remember meeting with a mom and her teenage daughter. The mom brought her daughter in, hoping I could halt her certain slide into a life of debauchery. It didn't take long to realize that the mom was the one with the problem. A self-proclaimed "wild child" who still struggled with many of the same issues of her youth, she read her own demons into everything her daughter did.

Every fashionable outfit signified a whore's wardrobe; every CD, a celebration of decadence. Movies were soft porn; potential suitors were sexual predators. She scrutinized everything her daughter said, did, saw, or read and then railed against most of it as titillating garbage.

With the daughter out of the room, I suggested that the mom back off. She was aghast. She called me soft on sin—and a few other things. From her vantage point, her bitter denunciations were the best way to literally scare the hell out of her daughter.

It never occurred to her that she was actually condemning herself rather than helping her daughter. A far better approach would have been to downshift her harsh condemnations in exchange for an honest discussion of her own struggles, her sordid past, and the scars those sins had left behind.

It might have caused her daughter to listen. I know God would have listened. And I'm sure that from his vantage point it would have been far better than what he had been hearing.

Deal with Our Own Stuff First

A second key to judging appropriately is to make sure that we deal with our own sins before we start worrying about everybody else's. Jesus didn't tell us to ignore the specks in the eyes of others. But he did tell us to take the log out of our own eye first. Then we'll be able to see clearly enough to help in taking the speck out of someone else's eye.[8]

That means that as long as I'm losing the battle over a specific sin in my own life, I need to keep my mouth shut. Not that I excuse or defend sin in others, but there's no wisdom in joining the chorus of those who are crusading against a particular sin when I have a closet full of my own sin.

This doesn't mean we have to be perfect. If that was so, then even the apostle Paul would have had to zip it.[9] Yet he clearly didn't. He was bold in his exposé of sin and error. We can be too, but not if a particular sin has us by the throat.

This principle is especially important to grasp for those of us who struggle with a secret sin that no one (or so we think) knows about. As long as the battle continues and the closet door remains shut, we have no right to be pointing out the public sins of others. To do so only makes matters worse. There are few lifelong secrets. Time has a way of revealing the things we've worked hardest to hide.

I watched this principle tragically unfold from a distance a number of years ago. It started when someone signed me up to receive a monthly publication from an ideologically conservative college. What caught my eye was the fervor with which the president of the college pummeled the evils and moral depravity of the so-called liberal left. He was what I call a pit bull for Jesus. Maybe you've known or come across a few of them yourself. If so, you know what I mean.

Frankly, I agreed with many (though not all) of the things he said. I, too, was alarmed by a host of cultural and political trends that seemed to be heading in the wrong direction. I shared many of the moral values he espoused. While I often failed to appreciate his tone, I had to admit that I resonated with much of the message.

Yet he would have been better off if he had never uttered a word or printed a single page. He had a closet full of garbage that rendered him unfit to speak or write, no matter how true his words may have been.

When the closet door was opened, it revealed a nineteen-year affair with his daughter-in-law. Obviously he lost everything: his job, his family, his credibility. On top of that, the opponents he worked so hard to defeat were emboldened. They had a heyday skewering his hypocrisy. And thanks to Google, he'll never be able to outrun or outlast the shame of his sin. It lingers forever out in the open, just a few short keystrokes and a click away.

But that's not the worst of it. The worst of it is that, according to the words of Jesus, God was taking notes. The harsh judgments this man had been so quick to dish out to others have now been turned back on him. I'll leave it to the theologians to sort out all the details of how that works out. In the meantime I'll stick with the big picture and the one thing I know for certain: public judgments make private sin that much worse. It's a foolish path to take.

Don't Judge If God Hasn't Spoken Clearly

A third key to judging rightly is to make sure that our judgments match God's. As we've already seen, the myth that God doesn't want us to judge can put us in the awkward position of disagreeing with God when he calls something sin and we're unwilling to do so. But there is also an opposite mistake when it comes to judging others. We can judge and rip on things God has no problem with.

It didn't take me long as a new Christian to realize that many of the harshest judgments I heard people make were often in areas where the Bible seemed to be less than clear. The fact is, there are many areas where the Scriptures lay down a general principle without spelling out all the specific applications. That leaves us with lots of freedom and latitude—and lots of areas for potential disagreement.

For instance, the Bible says that our bodies are the temple of the Holy Spirit and should be treated as such.[10] That's a principle. It's left to us to figure out how it applies. For some of us, that means avoiding cigarettes, cigars, and alcohol. For others, it means avoiding diet drinks and refined sugars. For still others, it means vigorous exercise and proper rest. For me, it means staying away from Spam, beets, and cauliflower.

But in the days of the New Testament, that verse specifically meant not having sex with a temple prostitute. Because that's probably not a problem for most of us today (have you seen any temple prostitutes in your neighborhood lately?), it's up to us to figure out how that principle still applies. There's room for differing applications.

We put ourselves in dangerous company when we judge others in an area where God has not spoken definitively. Like the Pharisees of old, we can end up pontificating about things God couldn't care less about, while missing the things he cares most about.

I learned long ago that anything left out of the Bible was not left out by mistake. God wasn't rushing to meet a publisher's deadline. He doesn't wish he had a more careful editor. He's not looking for a rewrite. Adding rules, regulations, standards, or anything else we wish he'd included, and then judging those who fail to follow our additions, puts us at odds with God. It also puts us at risk of being branded a spiritual liar, no matter how strongly we feel about an issue.[11]

Yet the more passionate we are about an issue, the harder it can be to let it go. Listen to our political rhetoric, our battles over obscure theological distinctives, and our rants against those who do church differently. By far, the harshest letters and e-mails I've ever received have been those triggered by a tradition, a preference, or a topic the writer felt so strongly about—and the Bible said nothing about.

This same tendency was noted by the apostle Paul in his letter to the church in Corinth. He chided them for their endless arguments and then said sarcastically, "Of course you have to fight over these things, or how else would you be able to prove your spiritual superiority over one another?"[12]

Back then, just as today, most of the fiercest divisions among Christians were not over things spelled out clearly in Scripture. Instead they were between competing factions over areas of interpretation where the Bible was silent, obscure, or granted freedom.

We seldom fight over things that are black and white—precisely because they are black and white. When the Scriptures are clear, there's not much room for disagreement. But when things are more nuanced—now we have something to "dialogue" about.

Christians and Non-Christians

Perhaps the most misunderstood aspect of judging biblically has to do with how we evaluate and judge the non-Christian world around us. It's here that many of us make a well-intentioned mistake. We judge non-Christians by Christian standards.

Usually it's an attempt to take a stand for righteousness. But judging non-Christians by Christian standards puts the cart before the horse. Even if we successfully convince non-Christians to live by Christian standards (or successfully legislate it), without bringing people into relationship with Christ, all we've done is populate hell with nicer and more moral people.[13]

More important, the Bible specifically forbids us to judge non-Christians by Christian standards.[14]

That doesn't mean that we can't call their sin, sin. It doesn't mean that they disobey God's law with impunity. It just means we're supposed to leave their judgment to him and focus on ourselves and the family of God when it comes to enforcing his standards.

■ ■ ■

We can learn much from the early Christians. They lived in a culture and under a government system riddled with what the Bible calls sin. Marriage was held in low esteem; sexual excess was tacitly approved; homosexuality was celebrated. Infanticide was an accepted form of family planning. The Colosseum was regularly filled with blood-thirsty crowds cheering the death of the vanquished. As for Christians, there were no charitable deductions, property tax exemptions, freedom of speech protections—just the ominous threat of a coming day when Christianity would be outlawed, believers jailed, and leaders martyred.

Yet the New Testament is strangely silent when it comes to harsh judgments and condemnations of Roman government, its leaders, or its soldiers. While it does speak of societal decadence in general, it usually does so in the context of reminding the Christians that they were no longer to live that way.

The reason was simple. The early church understood that their job was not to judge and condemn the pagans around them. Their job was to win them over.

Evaluate and Protect

If we refuse to judge, we miss out on truth. If we judge inappropriately, we pile extra judgment upon ourselves. Seems to me, this judging thing can be rather dangerous on both ends! Like the nuclear fuel at a power plant, it can bring great benefit if handled correctly, extract a high price if ignored, or hurt everyone if handled improperly.

A final key to balancing it all is to remember that our ultimate purpose is never to condemn. That's God's prerogative. Our role is to evaluate and protect or to discern and restore, depending upon the situation and the people involved.

Spiritual Leaders

When it comes to spiritual leaders (either self-proclaimed or widely acclaimed), the purpose of our judging is to evaluate and protect. The goal is to keep wolves in sheep's clothing from raiding the flock. So a leader's message, actions, and spiritual fruit are fair game.[15] If a spiritual leader's life or teaching fails to match up with the Scriptures, we help no one but the false prophet by keeping quiet or failing to point out the inconsistencies or errors of his or her ways.

But even so, it must be done with an eye to the principles of judgment we've already seen. We must remain humble, remembering our own failings. And we must only judge in those areas where God has spoken clearly.

As for our differences of opinion, style, or debatable theological distinctives, these are best left for God to arbitrate someday. And when that day comes, my bet is that he'll probably point out how much we all missed it, especially the part about patiently bearing with one another and forgiving as we've been forgiven.

Fellow Christians

In the case of judging our fellow Christians, the purpose is always to discern and restore. In contrast to the prohibition against judging non-Christians, we have a responsibility to judge and hold one another spiritually accountable. But the purpose is always to root out the sin or error in order to restore the one caught in its web.

Again, we must always look to ourselves first and avoid making judgments about things God doesn't spell out or care about. But when the Scriptures are clear, we can't ignore sin. Refusing to do so in an attempt to avoid being labeled as "judgmental" is not an act of grace; it's an act of disobedience.[16]

Judging with Grace

Finally, we must judge with grace. When our judgments lead us into personal attacks, bitterness, or raging anger, something has gone terribly wrong.[17]

The old cliché is right. Hate the sin and love the sinner.

But if you're anything like me, you've probably wondered how it's possible to hate one without hating the other. The sin and the sinner seem inexorably tied together, don't they?

Frankly, that cliché always struck me as a great sound bite but a practical impossibility. Until a friend pointed out that I was already doing it quite well in regard to one person.

Myself.

> *God wants us to judge in the same way we both judge and love ourselves—boldly calling sin, sin, while responding with an abundance of grace and mercy.*

He was right. I seldom have any problem hating my own sins while still loving myself. In fact, that's one of the primary reasons I hate my sins. They not only dishonor my Lord, but they also hurt and destroy me personally. And I hate to see that happen to a good guy like me.

This concept of self-love is so natural and deeply ingrained that Jesus used it as the basis for how we are to love others (and that includes our enemies and those who are advancing a sinful agenda).[18]

When it comes to judging them or anyone, God wants us to judge in the same way we both judge and love ourselves—boldly calling sin, sin, while responding with an abundance of grace and mercy. It's a myth that Christians shouldn't judge. We can and should. We just need to make sure we are judging the right things in the right way.

A proper understanding of when and how to judge is an important step toward spiritual maturity. Without it, we can end up at either one of two dangerous extremes: winking at sin in the mistaken belief that we have no right to judge the beliefs and actions of others or unintentionally condemning ourselves with our harsh denunciations of the very things we struggle with—or God could care less about.

CAN CHRISTIANS EVER JUDGE?

"Do not judge, or you too will be judged. For in the same way you judge others, you will be judged, and with the measure you use, it will be measured to you.

"Why do you look at the speck of sawdust in your brother's eye and pay no attention to the plank in your own eye? How can you say to your brother, 'Let me take the speck out of your eye,' when all the time there is a plank in your own eye? You hypocrite, first take the plank out of your own eye, and then you will see clearly to remove the speck from your brother's eye....

"Watch out for false prophets. They come to you in sheep's clothing, but inwardly they are ferocious wolves. By their fruit you will recognize them."

MATTHEW 7:1–5, 15–16

6
EVERYTHING HAPPENS FOR A REASON

A number of years ago, my wife was diagnosed with cancer. At the time, things looked grim. Choosing prayer support over privacy, we decided to keep our friends and congregation in the loop as to what was happening.

All in all, we're glad we did. But there were days when we weren't so sure. It wasn't the furtive glances or knowing nods that got us. It wasn't the whispers or sudden silence when we entered a room. It was the well-intentioned words of "encouragement" that nearly did us in.

Not that we didn't need some encouragement. Lord knows, we did. But a good portion of what people meant to be encouraging and helpful was in reality quite painful. It didn't make things better. It made things worse.

Like most people in a similar situation, we were inundated with articles, books, Web sites, special diets, and supplements, all of which came with a promise to heal or slow down the spread of the disease. They also came with a subtle but nonetheless clear message: "If you had followed this advice earlier, you wouldn't be in the jam you're in now."

We never did have the time or energy to read all the pamphlets, check out the Web sites, or try the supplements. But we did learn a valuable lesson. The apostle Paul knew exactly what he was talking about when he gave his simple advice for ministering to those in dire straits: weep with those who weep.[1]

Yet more disconcerting than all the unsolicited advice was the "happy talk" of those who tried to assure us that Nancy's cancer was a blessing in disguise, an essential part of God's great and wonderful plan for our life.

We never quite knew how to respond. If this was God's best, then he could save it for someone else. We were willing to take a pass. We also noticed that none of those who were so quick to proclaim it a blessing seemed very eager to get blessed the same way in their own life.

Their words varied, but the message was always the same: someday you'll be glad this happened. We were told…
- "God must be up to something."
- "God doesn't make mistakes."
- "You must be very special for God to trust you with this."
- "Won't it be great to see how God uses this?"
- "Isn't it good to know that everything happens for a reason?"

In one sense they were absolutely right. No matter what happens, God is in control. He's King of the universe. And he's good.

But that doesn't mean he's the direct cause of everything that happens. It doesn't mean that everything that happens is something he wants to happen. And it certainly doesn't mean that everything he allows is good.

God did not cause Lucifer to rebel, Eve to eat the forbidden fruit, or David to sleep with Bathsheba. He did not kill Abel, build the tower of Babel, or force the crowd to cry out for Barabbas. He didn't coerce the Roman soldiers into killing Jesus. Those who carried out these evil deeds bear full responsibility for their actions. They can't blame God.

Adam tried. It didn't fly. You can look it up.[2]

Where Did We Get This Idea Anyway?

Like most spiritual urban legends, the idea that God causes everything that happens comes from a combination of wishful thinking and a twisted interpretation of a few key Scriptures. In this case, one verse in particular—Romans 8:28—takes the spotlight.

No verse gets misquoted more often when it comes to trying to make sense out of life's trials. Christians and even non-Christians who have a nodding acquaintance with the Bible quote it more than all other verses combined. It's the favorite proof text for the everything-is-good-if-you-wait-long-enough crowd. It's plastered on coffee mugs, posters, greeting cards, and all kinds of Jesus junk.

It sounds good. It sells well.

But Romans 8:28 doesn't say or mean what most people think it does. It doesn't even apply to a large percentage of those who turn to it for comfort.

What Romans 8:28 Actually Says

Much of the confusion can be traced to the way Romans 8:28 was translated in the Shakespearean English of the King James Version: "We know that all things work together for good to them that love God, to them who are the called according to his purpose."

On the surface, that seems to imply that everything that happens is a part of God's greater plan, that life is like a giant jigsaw puzzle that will make sense once all the other pieces are in place. It appears to say that, given enough time, *everything* that happens will prove to have been good or necessary.

But that's an unfortunate translation. It may have been accurate in the early 1600s. I don't know. I never spoke Shakespearean English. But I do know that language changes over time. Four hundred years ago, "charity" meant love. Now it means giving money away. Forty-five years ago, when I called someone a dope, my mom washed my mouth out with soap. But when my kids call something dope, it's high praise.

> God can and will accomplish his good purposes no matter what. But that's a far cry from saying that everything that happens is somehow good or necessary.

A more accurate rendering of Romans 8:28 in modern English reads like this: "We know that in all things God works for the good of those who love him, who have been called according to his purpose."

Notice the difference. It doesn't say that everything that happens is good. It simply says that God is at work in all things.

In other words, even the enemy's best shot can't thwart God's ultimate plan. God can and will accomplish his good purposes no matter what. But that's a far cry from saying that everything that happens is somehow good or necessary.

Those who pin every disease, financial disaster, and betrayal on the direct action of God are headed down a logically indefensible path. If these things are really an expression of God's goodness, they would have shown up in the garden—before the Fall. They would surely play a prominent role in heaven, where God's goodness and blessings reign supreme. Yet that's clearly not the case.

Notice something else that most people miss. This verse is not a promise for everyone. It's not even a promise for every Christian. It's a promise for a specific kind of person, one who meets two important criteria. This verse is for someone who (1) loves God and (2) has been called according to his purpose.

So, who is that?

According to Jesus and the writers of the New Testament, those who love God are those who obey his commands. Those who are called according to his purpose are those who have become followers of Jesus.[3]

That leaves out a lot of people.

It leaves out the coworker in the cubicle down the hall who has no interest in spiritual things and just found out her youngest child has autism. God loves her. He has a preferred future for her (if and when she turns to Jesus). But Romans 8:28 has nothing to say to her present heartache.

It also leaves out the nice guy in the apartment next door (the one you've been witnessing to) who lost his job three weeks before his wedding. Assuring him that God must have something better in mind may make both of you feel better. But it's wishful thinking. God makes no such promise to those who fail to follow Jesus, no matter how nice they are.

It even leaves out some Christians. If we live in high-handed disobedience in some area of our life, there's no blanket promise that God will step in and fix the mess our defiance creates.

I once met with the parents of a pregnant teenager who came in to figure out how to best handle the situation. At one point they said, "We're not sure why God let this happen, but it's good to know he has a reason."

I didn't say anything. But I said to myself, *Unless we're dealing with another virgin birth here, God probably didn't have much to do with this deal.*

Unfortunately, they were so steeped in the urban legend of a God who allows only good things into our lives that it never entered their mind that this unborn child could be anything but a gift from the Lord. They knew their daughter shouldn't have been sleeping with her boyfriend. She knew it too. But now that she had repented, broken off the relationship, and turned back to God, he must have something good up his sleeve. Surely there was no way her child would turn out to be a source of heartache and frustration, a painful reminder of her sin.

I hoped they were right.

I prayed they were right.

But I could give them no assurance.

I've lived long enough to know that children aren't cute pets, single parenting is incredibly hard work, and the consequences of sin can be brutal even in the presence of God's mercy and grace.

Just ask David and Bathsheba. Sure, David was forgiven. Sure, he was used by God to write scripture after his sin. And yes, God brought some good out of their union, especially an amazing son named Solomon. But all in all, it would have been far better if he had never laid eyes on her. Their firstborn died in infancy. David spent the rest of his life at war. His family was a dysfunctional mess. None of which qualifies as God's wonderful plan for his life.

The same goes for a former drug addict friend of mine, now saved, struggling with the symptoms of hepatitis C. The onslaught of his disease is not a good thing. It's not God's blessing in disguise. It's the tragic consequence of past actions. Actions he now regrets. Actions he's been forgiven for—but actions he's paying for, in this life, just the same.

The beauty and promise of Romans 8:28 is not that the progression of his disease will eventually prove to be a good thing. It's that no matter how bad things may get, God's ultimate and eternal purpose in his life won't be foiled.

Don't Blame God

Those who assume that everything that happens has God's fingerprints all over it fail to distinguish between what God allows and what God causes—what God permits and what God prefers. The Bible makes it clear that there are a number of scenarios where the dark trials of our lives have nothing to do with God's wonderful plans for our lives.

Self-Inflicted Wounds

Sometimes the trials and hardships we face are the results of sinful choices. That's not God's doing. That's our doing.

I know a Christian family who lost their home to foreclosure. They took out a loan to buy a house they couldn't afford. Frankly, they got it by lying. Their broker told them to pad their income statement. He said, "Everybody does it." So they did.

Then when the economy faltered and all hell broke loose, a mutual friend stepped forward to tell them not to worry. They were in God's hands. He wouldn't let them down. They might lose their house, but he surely must have something better in mind.

It was false comfort.

The family had lied. It had caught up with them. God, indeed, had something better in mind. But it wasn't a nicer house. It was honesty—telling the whole truth even when it was inconvenient. Having failed to live up to God's Plan A, they were now forced to live with the consequences of Plan B.

Life in a Fallen World

Sometimes bad things happen because we live in a fallen world. To some degree, we're all caught in the backwash of Adam's sin. It's unavoidable. It's universal.[4]

I don't think it's a coincidence that the first story in the Bible after the fall of Adam and Eve is about a bad guy killing a good guy. That's what happens in a fallen world. Bad people do bad things and good people get hurt.

> *Any attempt to downplay the universal impact of the fall—or worse, the assumption that Christians have a magic bubble of protection— fails to square with Scripture. Or with life.*

Then there's Mother Nature. If you haven't noticed, she's been in a bad mood ever since Adam ate the forbidden fruit. Follow the news for a couple of weeks and you'll find plenty of examples of her arbitrary and malicious behavior. At times she's the ultimate mean girl.

And don't forget Murphy, her cousin. Also unleashed at the fall, he shows up uninvited (but regularly) just to mess things up. Adam knew him as the weeds in his garden. We know him as the reason why the other line always moves faster; why whatever can go wrong, does go wrong; why the later we are, the more traffic signals we hit. Murphy isn't God's emissary. He's Adam's legacy.

Any attempt to downplay the universal impact of the fall—or worse, the assumption that Christians have a magic bubble of protection—fails to square with Scripture. Or with life. It's a recipe for disappointment with God. When it comes to the consequences of the fall, we aren't offered immunity. We're offered eternity.[5]

Foolish Decisions

There is another reason bad stuff happens. Sometimes we make foolish decisions—not sinful decisions, just dumb ones.

We've all been there. Either we failed to check out the facts or we in some way put two and two together and got eight. No matter how or why it happens, once we've made a boneheaded decision, bad stuff usually follows.

Our choices matter. They have consequences. Picking the wrong stock can wipe out a portfolio. Picking the wrong partner can derail your business. Picking our nose can ruin our social status. It just happens.

It's ludicrous to blame God or to assume that he'll jump in and fix every idiotic decision we make. In fact, the Bible calls such thinking foolish.[6]

The good news isn't that God promises to keep us from making lame decisions or to fix whatever we break. It's that he promises to continue working for our eternal good no matter how many dimwitted judgments we make along the way.

Why This Is So Important

The belief that God is the direct cause of everything that happens (and has a specific reason and blessing for it) is not only untrue; it has the potential to produce great spiritual harm. Here are just a few of its most significant potential negative consequences.

Anger at God

In many cases, pinning everything on God leads to an unjustified anger at God. Most of us know someone who wants nothing to do with Jesus or Christianity primarily because of an injustice or great tragedy for which he or she blames God.

When we proclaim God as the direct cause of everything that happens, we unintentionally hand the enemy some powerful ammo. Ammo he'll gladly use to slander God's reputation. His argument usually goes something like this: "If God is responsible for your mess, he's obviously not very good or not very powerful. Why waste your time following a God like that?"

It's an accusation that rings true for many who have suffered, especially those saddled with the heavy burden of injustice or the oppressive weight of a major tragedy. Yet, ironically, the core belief that fuels their bitterness is the same belief that provides great comfort to those who see God's hand and blessing behind every tragedy. *Both see God as directly responsible for everything.*

The difference is in how they interpret what happens.

The everything-will-eventually-prove-to-be-good crowd judges what happens in light of their previous convictions about God's goodness. The God-can't-be-trusted crowd judges God's goodness in light of what actually happened. It's no surprise that they draw widely divergent conclusions.

Glossing over Sin

Another unintended consequence of assuming a God-ordained reason lies behind everything that happens is a glossing over of sin. Let's
be real. There's not much reason to fear sin or its consequences if
everything comes out in the wash anyway.

I've been told that an affair was part of God's plan because the new
union resulted in a happy marriage. I've been told God must have
orchestrated a bitter church split because it led to the birth of a dynamic
ministry. I've even been told that God was behind a murder and the
subsequent conviction because the murderer met the Lord in prison.

Such thinking is nonsense. God never approved of these people's
sin. He didn't cause it. He didn't even "use it." He overcame it. That's
what grace does.

Irresponsibility

This spiritual urban legend, when taken to an extreme, can also lead
to an epidemic of irresponsibility. After all, if God guarantees that
everything will eventually work out for good no matter what, who
cares what I put into the equation? God will patch it up. He has to.
He's promised.

I've watched such thinking produce a pattern of ridiculous risk
taking, conveniently labeled as steps of faith. Yet, most of the time,
my friends' so-called steps of faith (whether it was taking a huge
financial risk, ditching their career to move across country, or simply
putting all their chips on red) had nothing to do with following
God's leading. He hadn't told anyone to specifically do anything. But
no matter, like the fool in Proverbs, my friends ignored the warning
signs of danger and the advice of prudent friends and kept on going,
confident that if things didn't work out, God would bail them out.[7]

Sadly, when he didn't, some of them railed at God. But it's wasn't

God's fault for not coming through—it was their fault for running through a plethora of warning signs that should have caused any sensible person to come to a screeching halt.[8]

Misplaced Hope

Still another downside is the unrealistic expectations and misplaced hope that this idea tends to produce, particularly among those of us faced with long-term suffering.

I remember the question-and-answer session that followed a talk I gave on "Where's God When All Hell Breaks Loose?" A mother of a severely handicapped young boy stood up. Her son suffered from life-threatening seizures, often occurring daily.

At first she seemed to push back on the idea that God might not be the direct instigator of all that was happening to her son. She claimed it gave her purpose, meaning, and strength to see her son's condition as God's plan for her life.

Then she suddenly started to sob—deep, gut-wrenching sobs. Her next words revealed the dark side of her paradigm: a crushing disillusionment with God. "When will he fix this?" she cried out. "I can't take it anymore. Why doesn't he answer?"

Armed with the conviction that her son's condition was God's doing and would somehow prove to be a good thing in the long run, she was banking on an earthly miracle she would probably never see instead of setting her hope on the eternal inheritance that she and her son were guaranteed to see.

She was caught in an emotional quandary. As long as she saw God as the direct cause of her son's seizures, there was the possibility that he would stop the seizures. In that, she found great hope. But if he was the direct cause of the seizures, he was also the author of her son's private hell. In that, she found great despair.

Can a Bad Thing Ever Be a Good Thing?

Obviously there are situations where God takes something bad and uses it to produce something good. The ultimate example is the crucifixion of Jesus Christ.

Another case can be found in the misfortunes of Joseph and his subsequent rise to power in Egypt. God was obviously at work behind the scenes when Joseph was auctioned off by his own brothers, falsely accused of attempted rape, jailed, primed for early release, summarily forgotten, and finally brought before Pharaoh to interpret a bizarre dream.

When Joseph's brothers eventually came to ask him for mercy despite their despicable act of selling him into slavery, he responded with these famous words: "You intended to harm me, but God intended it for good to accomplish what is now being done, the saving of many lives."[9]

Many have seen in these words support for the notion that whatever happens to us, it's always a part of God's plan to bring about something better. But notice that Joseph didn't call his brothers' evil actions good or necessary. He didn't say that everything happens for a reason. He simply pointed out that God was at work despite their evil intents.

With 20/20 hindsight, it's easy to see that God used the brothers' sin to position Joseph for a high post in Egypt's royal court. In the process, God provided food for Joseph's father and brothers and put them in a setting where a small nomadic clan could grow into a great nation.

Yet there's no indication that the strength and integrity with which Joseph endured his injustices were based on an underlying belief that God was up to something special. Joseph had no clue. He just knew that righteousness was the path to take and would one day be rewarded, either in this life or eternity.

The fact is, just as it was for Joseph, it's nearly impossible for us to distinguish which of the painful events in our life result from God's orchestration, which ones he is planning to use, and which ones he'll overcome in eternity.

In the meantime it doesn't really matter. Every trial or hardship calls for the same response: obedience. We are to do the right thing no matter what the outcome. Sometimes, as in the case of Joseph, our obedience will be rewarded in this life. Sometimes it will be rewarded in the next. Only time will tell.

If God Is Going to Fix Things Someday, Why Not Now?

All of this raises a question. If some of the things that happen in our world aren't what God wants, why doesn't he step in and take charge? Why doesn't he shut down evil and be done with it? Why sit back and allow a defeated enemy to function as the god of this age?[10]

The answer is straightforward. God lingers because for every day he delays, more of his former enemies become his friends and family.[11]

Theologians will argue about the logistics and details of Jesus's return until he shows up. But all sides agree that when he finishes his work, evil will be history. Satan will be done. And those who have ignored God or chosen the path of rebellion will be out of second chances.

So, do you really want Jesus to come back and take charge tomorrow?

I don't.

I still have too many friends and loved ones who don't know the

Lord. Some are almost there. Some are on the fence. Some are no-where close. But every day Jesus holds off returning, he gives these friends of mine another opportunity to submit to his reign. Once he shows up, that chance will be lost forever.

In the meantime I'll gladly put up with consequences of living in a fallen world, the backwash of the bad things evil people do, the harsh moods of Mother Nature, and even the painful consequences of my own sin and folly. I want him to come back—just not *too* quickly. I'd rather he wait until more of my friends and loved ones step over the line.

Apparently, so far he feels the same way.

Silver Lining or Path of Obedience?

One more thing I've noticed. Those who insist that God directly orchestrates everything for an ultimately good purpose spend a lot of time looking for that purpose. No matter what happens, they're always searching for the silver lining. And even when it's not there, they seem to find it. It reminds me of a friend of mine who always finds a funny face in the clouds even when the rest of us can't see it.

Psychologically and emotionally, that might appear to be a good thing to do. After all, it can help us keep a positive outlook. But the benefits are only a mirage leading to disappointment and disillusionment when the harsh truth of reality sets in.

When life falls apart, there's something far more important to look for than a silver lining. Once again, it's the path of obedience.

The path of obedience always takes the high road. It tells the truth even if the truth brings pain. It refuses to return evil for evil, even when vengeance is within reach. It's thankful, even when there's not much to be thankful for. It walks with integrity, even when no one else does. It does the right thing, even when the right thing doesn't work out so well.

> *When life falls apart, there's something far more important to look for than a silver lining. It's the path of obedience.*

Bottom line: God hasn't promised that everything will always "work out" in this life. But he has promised that, no matter what happens, he will never leave nor forsake us.[12] In Romans 8:28 he's also promised that no matter what life or the enemy might throw our way, God's good and eternal purposes can never be thwarted.

But please, let's stop calling the devil's best shot God's doing. Let's stop calling Adam's legacy God's handiwork. And let's stop calling evil good.

It helps out no one but the enemy.

By the Way

My wife and I found a way to respond to the well-intentioned but hurtful attempts at "encouragement" during her cancer.

One day, after reading a particularly insensitive e-mail from someone I knew was only trying to help, it hit me that when our kids were young they had often done the same thing. On virtually every Hallmark holiday, they would give us something that was frankly rather ugly, at least to anyone who couldn't see the heart behind it. Sometimes it was a bouquet of mismatched flowers and dandelions from the yard. Sometimes it was a picture that looked more like a Rorschach inkblot than anything else. Sometimes it was a belt or paperweight picked up at their school's rummage sale. Almost always it was something we didn't want or need.

But that didn't matter. To us, it was always a thing of beauty because of the intent behind it. It's what made a wilted bouquet worthy of a fine vase and made a garage sale paperweight a treasured keepsake.

In the same way, once we learned to look beyond the occasional ugliness of the words people said about my wife's cancer to the beauty of the heart behind it (and the message they were *trying* to convey), it changed everything.

It made some painful words bearable, some ugly stuff not so ugly. But one thing it couldn't do. It never made her cancer a good thing or a blessing in disguise.

DOES EVERYTHING HAPPEN FOR A REASON?

We know that in all things God works for the good of those who love him, who have been called according to his purpose....

No, in all these things we are more than conquerors through him who loved us. For I am convinced that neither death nor life, neither angels nor demons, neither the present nor the future, nor any powers, neither height nor depth, nor anything else in all creation, will be able to separate us from the love of God that is in Christ Jesus our Lord.

ROMANS 8:28, 37–39

7 LET YOUR CONSCIENCE BE YOUR GUIDE

I used to do a lot of counseling. Every week I'd meet with a steady stream of individuals and couples who were trying to work their way through the deep weeds of life. They'd come in. I'd listen. I'd ask a few questions. Then I would listen some more. After a while, if I thought I had the situation sized up, I'd offer some advice or provide some perspective. Or if I had no answers, I'd empathize.

Sometimes it helped.

Sometimes it didn't.

That's how counseling works.

But there was one type of person I never did find a way to help. Thankfully, they didn't show up in large numbers. But when they did show up, I had no idea what to say. You'd think they would have eventually figured it out and passed on the message "Don't go to Larry. He's clueless!" But they didn't. They kept coming anyway, hopeful that I'd be able to help them untangle the messes they found themselves in, despite all the evidence to the contrary.

Who were these impossible-to-help-but-desperate-for-help folks?

They were church members who came in with enormous problems created by their own foolish or evil behavior—but who adamantly insisted that none of it was their fault, because they'd done nothing wrong.

There's not much left to talk about when somebody comes in with a self-inflicted wound and demands, "Fix this. I'm in a mess. It's not my fault. I did nothing wrong." I mean, where do you go from there?

I never did figure it out.

Taking on the IRS

One man came in with his marriage on fumes and the feds on his trail. Years before, he had attended a seminar that convinced him that the IRS and federal income taxes were illegal and unconstitutional. So he stopped paying taxes and took up the crusade.

By the time we met, the government was closing in. His bank accounts had been seized, his paychecks garnished. To put food on the table, he was working as a day laborer (on a cash-only basis), trying to hide and survive in the underground economy. His wife, who had previously acquiesced to his theories and actions, was angry, panicked, and threatening divorce.

As he laid out his rationale and the details of his actions, I was stunned. It didn't fit. I'd known him and his wife for more than a year. They attended our church faithfully. His occasional probing questions after a sermon had led me to believe that he was a strong Christian with a high regard for Scripture.

So I figured a good place to start would be an overview of what the Bible had to say about paying taxes.

Boy, was I wrong.

After we looked at several passages that clearly exhort Christ followers to submit to governing authorities and pay their taxes, he blew me off.

"You don't get it," he said as he pointed to his seminar notebook and an enormous file of supporting arguments and articles. "The IRS has no legal grounds to take our money. If you pay them, you're supporting an illegal practice and a corrupt government. How can you justify that?"

I decided to show him more verses, this time pointing out that Jesus paid taxes he was technically exempt from and Paul encouraged his readers to pay taxes earmarked for the godless Roman Empire.[1] But it was to no avail. I think I could have shown him a thousand verses. They would have done no good.

Jiminy Cricket

It didn't matter what the courts, legal experts, the Bible, or anyone else said. This tax evader had no qualms, either legally or morally about his actions. On a scale of one to ten, he scored a twelve in degree of certainty. He was absolutely sure he had done nothing wrong—for one simple reason.

He had bought into the Jiminy Cricket code of ethics. He trusted his own conscience above all else. He was convinced that it was his best and most trustworthy guide to morality. As long as he had a clear conscience and a sense of inner peace about his decision, the matter was closed.

"Ultimately," he told me, "I have to let my conscience be my guide. After all, isn't that why God gave me one?"

"Well," I told him, "not really."

The Myth of a Trustworthy Conscience

I tell his story because most of us have a hard time imagining how anyone could be so foolish. Because we can't envision ourselves ignoring an abundance of court decisions and crystal-clear scriptures to take on the federal government in an obviously futile battle, we write him off as an idiot.

But not so fast.

You and I have probably made many of our own decisions and moral judgments using almost the same rationale and core assumptions as my tax-dodging friend. It's just that we've applied them to a different set of data and issues.

Like Tax Dodger, many of us have been taught to trust our conscience as a God-given, internal indicator of right and wrong. Faced with a tough moral dilemma, we turn to it. If we have peace about our decision or action (read that as an absence of guilt), we assume it must be okay. Otherwise, our conscience would surely have let us know something was wrong.

But such thinking reflects a fundamental misunderstanding of the role of our conscience and how it actually functions. The idea that our conscience is a trustworthy moral guide is a myth. It's another spiritual urban legend that, though widely believed, finds no support in either Scripture or the way life really works.

Thermometers and Thermostats

The problem is that a lot of us imagine our conscience to be a spiritual thermometer. We assume it can be placed into any situation and it will tell us the moral temperature—too hot, too cold, or just right. But that's not how our conscience works. It isn't a spiritual thermometer. It's a spiritual thermostat.

The difference is important. Thermostats don't define hot or cold. They reflect our definitions of hot and cold. We set them to respond however we like.

My wife and I, like many couples, have two widely different definitions of "comfortable." When I think it's stuffy, she complains it's too cold. What I call fresh air she calls an arctic blast. So it's no surprise that we often find ourselves engaged in a game of thermostat tug of war.

That's why I thought I had died and gone to heaven when we bought a car with dual climate zones. No more "compromises." No more sneaky adjustments when the other person wasn't looking. We could each set our personal thermostat to our own liking and then sit back and enjoy the ride.

I usually set mine somewhere between 70 and 72 degrees. If the temperature on my side moves above that, the air conditioner kicks in.

> *Our conscience doesn't tell us if we're violating God's standards. It tells us when we're violating our standards.*

But on the other side of the car, it's a different story. Nancy sets her thermostat at 74 degrees (or maybe it's 80 degrees—I don't know; I just know it's hot enough to cook oatmeal). So when her side gets too hot for my comfort, nothing happens. Her thermostat just sits there.

Now, suppose I took my car back to the dealer to complain

about Nancy's side of the car heating up. The mechanic would be puzzled. No doubt he'd point out that that's how thermostats are designed to work. They don't define hot and cold. *We* define hot and cold. They just respond to our definitions.

That's exactly how our conscience works. It's a spiritual thermostat. We set it to the standards we choose. We determine when it kicks in and when it stays idle. It doesn't tell us if we're violating *God's* standards. It tells us when we're violating *our* standards.

Seesaw Morality

Our conscience is also easy to reset. Just take a look in life's rearview mirror. Most of us (perhaps all of us) can identify actions and attitudes that we once thought to be wrong but that now produce not the slightest twinge of guilt. The same goes for some things we once approved of but now frown upon.

I first became aware of how pliable my own conscience was during my first few years as a Christian. After a radical turn to faith, I wanted to do everything I could to follow God's leading. It wasn't long until I began to make some significant lifestyle changes that aligned with the new values and standards I was supposedly learning from the Bible.

One problem, though. Lots of the things I was told were from the Bible weren't actually found in the Bible. You see, some of my earliest spiritual mentors were legalists. They had lots of rules. Some came from the Bible. Most didn't. But I was too new at this Jesus thing to know the difference. In my zeal to follow God, I took everything they said to heart.

As a result, my newly sensitized conscience began to trouble me about lots of things that had never bothered me before. I felt guilty not only when I was tempted to lie or cheat but also whenever someone broke out a deck of cards, checked out a movie, listened to rock music or—horror of horrors—danced to it, or otherwise participated in a host of endeavors that I'd been told were "worldly."

My spiritual thermostat had been reset to a whole new calibration. But it didn't stay there long.

As I continued to grow in my faith and started to read the Bible for myself—and started to understand what I was reading—I discovered that much of what I'd been trained to feel guilty about didn't match up with Scripture. I was shocked to learn that Jesus made a mean Merlot, that a harsh and judgmental spirit was more dangerous than a deck of playing cards, that God was more concerned about what was in my heart than what was in my refrigerator.

The result was another major realignment of my conscience.

Yet, for a while, I was more confused than ever. I now had three standards vying for my allegiance: my old pre-Christian values, my recent legalistic values, and my new what-does-the-Bible-actually-say values.

Even though I'd turned my back on the legalistic teaching of my early mentors, their voices still whispered in my ear. At the same time, my new insights from Scripture beckoned me in another direction. Frankly, much of the time, I had no idea if my thoughts and convictions came from the Holy Spirit, the nudging of my conscience, or merely an old tape that was still playing in my head.

My bet is that you've experienced some of these same seesaw shifts of conscience. Nearly everyone does. And that alone should give us great pause before trusting our conscience as a reliable barometer of spirituality and ethics. It's far too pliable to be counted on as an absolute authority.

But there are other dangers that lurk in the shadows, other

powerful reasons why it's never a good idea to let our conscience be our guide or to trust it as the final arbitrator of right and wrong—even when we think we've carefully aligned it with Scripture.

More Reasons Why Our Conscience Can't Be Trusted

Perhaps the most telling passage in the Bible regarding the inadequacy of our conscience is found in 1 Corinthians 4:3–4. In this passage the apostle Paul defends his ministry motivation and methods to a group of critics. What he says about his conscience is astounding. "I care very little if I am judged by you or by any human court; indeed, I do not even judge myself. My conscience is clear, but that does not make me innocent. It is the Lord who judges me."

The first time I read this passage, I was stunned. I mean, how could the apostle Paul not be satisfied with a clear conscience? If anyone could count on his conscience being aligned with Scripture and God's value system, it would have been the apostle Paul. He didn't just know the Bible; he was writing large sections of it!

But the more I considered his words within the larger context of Scripture, the more they made sense. He had lots of good reasons not to trust in his conscience as his final arbitrator. So do we.

See if you don't agree.

Our Sin Nature and Blind Spots

Since Adam's fall, we've all been born with what theologians call a sin nature. Becoming a follower of Christ provides us with the power to overcome it, but it doesn't eradicate it. As every longtime Christian knows, it's not a battle that's won overnight. It's a stage-by-stage process, with some significant setbacks along the way.

To make matters worse, our sin nature doesn't just show up as a desire to live selfishly and do wrong things. It also shows up in the way we think. In other words, it clouds everything, including our understanding of spiritual truth and God's leading.

That explains why two Christians who are equally committed to God and desiring to know his leading can come to diametrically opposite conclusions about what God wants. Our sin nature puts static on the line and afflicts all of us with our own unique spiritual blind spots. The bummer is that we don't always recognize the static and we never know where the blind spots are. (That's why they're called blind spots.)

The apostle Paul was no different.

Here was a man who knew what it was like to walk in the Spirit, to receive divine visitations, to experience miraculous healing power, to know the mind of God well enough to write the Word of God. But at that same time he struggled with his own sins and had to wage a constant battle with the same powerful enemy within that we do.[2]

At various points in his apostolic tenure, he misread the leading of the Lord, prayed for things God didn't want him to have, grew discouraged, and even despaired of life. He also failed to offer the same grace and second chance he'd received (when one of his young helpers bailed in the middle of a tough mission trip), had a bitter split with his main mentor, trusted untrustworthy people, and planted some pretty dysfunctional churches (which is why he had to write all those New Testament letters).[3]

In other words, he was thoroughly human. Completely saved, amazingly used, a spiritual giant—but thoroughly human nonetheless. And it was his recognition of his humanity and fallen nature that caused him not to put too much trust in his clear conscience.

I figure, if an apostle didn't fully trust his own conscience, I ought not put too much stock in mine. Wouldn't you agree?

Bad Software

There's still another danger that comes with letting our conscience be our guide. Like a computer, our conscience is no better than the data it relies upon. Sadly, it can be subjected to some pretty lame programming. And since our conscience is no more trustworthy than the standard it's calibrated to, we can end up feeling very good about some very bad things.

As I mentioned earlier, before I became a Christian, I lived by a set of moral values that I now know to be faulty. Then when I stepped over the line to follow Christ, those values were replaced by another set of goofy ideas from my legalist friends. In each case I thought I was living by the truth. But I wasn't. My conscience was badly out of whack. It was like having a GPS unit with all the software messed up. It confidently told me where to go and what to do, but most of what it told me was wrong. As a result, I made some dumb (and sinful) decisions that were nonetheless accompanied by a completely clear conscience.

To make matters worse, like many people, I took most of my moral cues from those around me. I assumed the majority couldn't be wrong. And if they were, God would surely understand. But that too was foolish. Majority doesn't equal morality. God nowhere promises that if enough people take the wrong path, he'll turn it into the right path. In fact, a case could be made that the best way to determine God's will or the right course of action is to take an opinion poll and then do the exact opposite.

Yet, the powerful influence and the gravitational pull of the majority are hard to break, which leaves lots of us with a misinformed and poorly programmed conscience. Now, if we add to that the false teachers and misled mentors we occasionally allow into our life, and our susceptibility to spiritual blind spots, it becomes obvious why the Jiminy Cricket code of ethics—letting our conscience be our guide—might not be such a great idea after all.

A Callused Heart

There is one more characteristic of our conscience that makes it dangerous to rely on. Over time, it can become callused. Now, a callus isn't a bad thing if you are a guitar player or a distance runner. It allows you to play for hours or run for miles once you've lost your normal sensitivity to pain.

But a callused conscience is a different matter. Once our conscience loses its sensitivity, it's not good for much.

Most of us have experienced the callusing of our conscience to some degree. Think back to something you felt guilty about the first time you did it. If you kept at it, most likely your sense of guilt began to dissipate. Keep at it long enough and the guilt goes away for good. That can leave us with a clear conscience. But it doesn't mean our actions are praiseworthy. It just means our conscience has been desensitized to the point where it no longer responds when prompted.

To make matters worse, once our conscience has been heavily callused toward a particular action, it becomes almost impossible for us to understand what all the fuss is about when others try to point out the error of our way. We simply no longer get it. Our ability to feel guilt is gone.

I once met with a man in our church (I'll call him Nick) who'd come to Christ a few years earlier. We were meeting because it had come to light that he had a massive porn stash. To my surprise, he was incredulous that his new wife or any of us at the church saw anything wrong with his "erotic" collection.

"Every guy has one," he told me. And he meant it. He really did.

As we talked, it became obvious that Nick had a long-term and deep-seated sexual addiction. His friends in his pre-Christian background saw nothing wrong with porn, and his current coworkers saw nothing wrong with it either. From his vantage point, porn was something every guy watched—he just had a better collection than most.

At first I was dumbfounded. How could he feel absolutely no shame or guilt? I thought perhaps a closer look at the truth and some clear-cut Scriptures might lead to a breakthrough. After all, this man was a self-proclaimed Christian.

But the more we talked, the clearer it became. His conscience wasn't misinformed. It was callused. No information, Bible verse, or spiritual truth would change his mind. He had built up too thick a callus for that. His years of ignoring the shouts, then the plaintive cries, and finally the last-gasp whispers of his conscience had left him incapable of feeling even a twinge of guilt. All he had left was justification of his sin.

Eventually I asked him to take me back to his first recollection and experience with pornography. He said it was as a seventh grader, when he stumbled upon a pile of his dad's magazines. And sure enough, when pushed, he finally admitted that he did indeed feel dirty and ashamed the first few times he leafed through them. But it wasn't long until the feelings of shame began to dissipate, overwhelmed by the excitement of the sexual charge and release that accompanied his ever-more-frequent forays into his dad's closet.

Now, years later, porn had become an accepted part of his life. He not only didn't feel guilty—he couldn't imagine why anyone would.

Here's the kicker. In every other area of Nick's life, it appeared that God had done some major housecleaning. When it came to matters of mercy and justice, he was spot on. When it came to having a heart for serving others, he was first in line. When it came to honesty and integrity, he couldn't bear the slightest misrepresentation. And as he pointed out with pride, he tithed off the gross.

When I asked Nick how he rationalized his use of hard-core pornography in light of the Bible studies and sermons he'd heard for the past three years, he told me that I was just toeing the party line, that he and I both knew no one really believed that stuff. In fact, he assumed I had my own stash or at least a few favorite Web sites.

When we insisted that he step down from his volunteer post and tightened the screws of accountability, Nick bolted. I never did see him again.

Admittedly, Nick's is an extreme example of a callused conscience. Perhaps the most callused one I've ever come across. But having dealt with hundreds of lesser versions of the same thing, I've come to the conclusion that lots of people who want to let their conscience be their guide have no idea that it's no longer working very well.

Just check out any prison. You'll find that it's filled with people who let their conscience be their guide—with dire consequences. But, sadly, we can find the same thing in many of our churches.

> *Just check out any prison. You'll find that it's filled with people who let their conscience be their guide—with dire consequences. But, sadly, we can find the same thing in many of our churches.*

I think of some businesspeople I know who no longer give a second thought to breaking their word (or the law) to make a deal work or to close a sale. They tell me that's what they have to do to succeed. They write off those who object as idealistic fools as they continue to pass out their business cards with a little fish in the corner.

I think of the "functional" drunks and "recreational" potheads I've known who staunchly defended their right to "relax" as long as they didn't hurt anybody—oblivious to the pain of those closest to them as it destroyed their marriage, family, or career.

Or how about the huge numbers of Christian couples who claim that sexual purity is unrealistic and restrictions against living together are "old school"?

All of these folks have one thing in common. They defend their actions as appropriate. They're convinced that God understands, if not outright approves. Most really mean it. Their consciences are genuinely clear. But most of the time, their consciences are only clear because they're no longer working.

So, What's It Good For?

All this raises a question. If our conscience is so undependable, what's it good for?

> *When rightly understood and functioning properly, our conscience is a valuable early warning device.*

To begin with, it's a great early warning system. Unless it's been neglected and ignored to the point of developing a thick callus, it reliably informs us when we're about to violate *our own* moral standards. Though our standards may or may not be aligned with God's, there is still great value in knowing we're about to do something we would consider questionable in our saner moments. Its prompting to stop and reconsider can save lots of heartache, especially since every journey into the abyss starts with a few small steps into the canyon.

Our conscience's ease of adjustment can also be a good thing. That means we have the ability to constantly realign it to Scripture if we so choose. The more accurately we do so, the greater our ability to recognize and avoid the deceptive lures of sin.[4]

When rightly understood and functioning properly, our conscience is a valuable early warning device. Like a yellow or red traffic light, it tells us to slow down, be cautious, or slam on the brakes. And when it does so, it's time to check the Scriptures before proceeding.

But it's a terrible green light. And this is where those who let their conscience be their definitive guide and ultimate arbitrator of right or wrong get into the most trouble. As we've already seen, even apostles didn't take a clear conscience as assurance of God's approval. We shouldn't either.

SHOULD OUR CONSCIENCE BE OUR GUIDE?

My conscience is clear, but that does not make me innocent. It is the Lord who judges me. Therefore judge nothing before the appointed time; wait till the Lord comes. He will bring to light what is hidden in darkness and will expose the motives of men's hearts. At that time each will receive his praise from God.

1 CORINTHIANS 4:4–5

The heart is deceitful above all things and beyond cure. Who can understand it?

JEREMIAH 17:9

8
GOD BRINGS
GOOD
LUCK

As a pastor, I like to hang around the front of the church after a worship service in order to be available for anyone who wants to talk. It beats hiding backstage like a rock star or standing by an exit in a quasi-receiving line.

It's always an interesting experience. I never know what to expect. Sometimes I get lots of questions. Other times it's prayer requests, attaboys, or a debate over a theological nuance. Sometimes the lines are long. Sometimes they're so short I wonder if I have cooties.

But one thing is consistent. The people who make the effort to come up and talk are often dealing with serious issues. They tend to get right to the point. There's not a lot of God talk or Christianese. No one seems to worry much about social protocol or making a good impression when all hell has just broken loose. The conversations are often raw, blunt, forceful, and even emotional.

Most of the time, I love it. It's why I went into ministry. But I have to admit there are times when it's overwhelming. Sometimes I wish I had a greenroom to hide in or an innocuous receiving line to stand in. It sure would beat having to deal with people like Tim.

■ ■ ■

Tim showed up on a day when the line to talk was unusually long. As I worked my way through it, I noticed him standing off to the side. He was obviously anxious to get to me, but just as obviously, he was posturing to make sure he was the last one in line. That caught my attention because whenever people angle to be last in line, it's hardly ever a good sign. It usually means they're facing a particularly messy situation—or they're upset about something and I'm about to be on the receiving end of an angry tirade.

In Tim's case, his steely gaze, crossed arms, and tense body language gave it away. He was angry. So when his turn finally came, I braced myself, wondering what I or someone in the church had done to make him so irate.

But to my surprise, he wasn't angry at me or anything that had happened at church. He was angry at God. Actually, he was incensed at God. And as soon as I said, "Hey, what's up?" he let loose.

Tim's Tirade

"Bleep your bleeping God!" he exclaimed. "I'm done. Your Jesus hasn't done me a bit of good. I've tried to clean up my act. I even tried your damn tithing thing. It doesn't work. I just lost my job. My wife needs surgery, and now I don't have any insurance. Where's your bleeping God when we need him?"

Then he just stood there—staring me down, arms crossed.

At first I wasn't sure how to respond. I didn't know what he was looking for. Was his locker-room language supposed to shock me? Did he think I'd have some profound answer? Was his cold stare an attempt to engage me in a junior-high stare down?

I had no clue. But I was sure of one thing. He had no interest in entering into a rational discussion of his situation and the role that following Jesus might or might not have played in it.

After a lengthy and awkward pause, I decided to let him win the stare-down contest. I said something to him, though I have no recollection of what it was. (After all, his words were far more memorable and colorful than mine.) He then spouted off more of the same as I tried to calm him down. But it did no good. He obviously just wanted to vent. After a few more expletives, he finally turned and stormed out.

I never saw him again.

At first glance it might appear that Tim's angry outburst was triggered by the series of tough breaks and unfortunate events that had engulfed his life. But in reality that's not what caused him to go off. Lots of people face similar and far worse scenarios without blasting God or anyone else.

No, what lit his fuse was a set of unfounded and unrealistic expectations about what it means to follow God and what should happen when we venture to do so. He thought living life God's way would bring him good fortune. He assumed that God would reach down and tip the scales his way, that life would be better and easier than before. When the opposite happened, he felt ripped off. God had promised him one thing and then delivered another.

Does God Bring Good Luck?

But Tim had it all wrong. The Bible makes no such promise. While there are some verses that speak of righteousness bringing about temporal blessings, reading these in the context of the Scripture as a whole, a strong case can be made that following God is just as likely (if not more likely) to bring bad luck than good—at least in the short run.[1]

As for Jesus, he certainly never promised his followers a long run of good luck or earthly success. He promised forgiveness. He promised eternity. But winning lottery numbers, job promotions, good health, and riches?

Not exactly.

Unless you consider carrying a cross and being misunderstood, persecuted, hated, beaten, and killed a sign of good luck and success. And if that's the case, it might be a good idea to line up a counseling appointment as soon as possible.

A Common and Ancient Myth

While Tim's choice of adjectives was unusual, his assumptions about God were not. Lots of us feel the same way. We expect that living God's way should cause most things to work out (read that as good fortune). We also assume that high-handed rebellion against God should cause life to fall apart.

> *Jesus promised forgiveness. He promised eternity. But winning lottery numbers, job promotions, good health, and riches? Not exactly.*

But clearly that's not always how life works, which is what makes the idea that God brings good luck another in a long line of spiritual urban legends. On the surface it makes sense. It sounds reasonable. It's what we'd all like to believe.

But it's simply not true.

By the way, we're not the first ones to be bamboozled by this myth. It has a long history of misleading God's people. It's why Job's wife told him to curse God and die after her husband's horrendous run of bad luck. It's why Job's friends were convinced that he must have done something terribly wrong to bring such misfortune into his life.[2]

Perhaps the most powerful articulation of the pain and confusion this myth brings can be found in a document written thousands of years ago by an Israeli frustrated over the success of the wicked and the long-running misfortune of those who were attempting to live God's way. His name was Asaph and his thoughts weren't all that different from Tim's—though his choice of words was far more appropriate. "Surely in vain have I kept my heart pure; in vain have I washed my hands in innocence. All day long I have been plagued; I have been punished every morning."[3] But before turning his back on God (which he says elsewhere he was sorely tempted to do), Asaph did something that neither Tim nor Job's distraught wife ever did. He sought understanding. He took his complaints to God and waited for an answer.

Then one day, as he entered the sanctuary of God, it hit him. For the first time he fully grasped the eternal destiny of the wicked. He saw their sudden and terrible end. Suddenly his plight didn't seem so unfair or his deal so bad.[4]

Spitting into the Wind

It's understandable why so many of us would assume that being on God's side should bring good luck and success. It just makes sense. Only an idiot spits into the wind. Only a fool takes on God. We expect those who do so to quickly pay the price. For most of us, it's hard to fathom why God would sit back and allow the wicked to prosper while they mock him and hassle his people. We wouldn't allow it if we were God. So, why should he?

But clearly that's what he does sometimes. And if we start with the assumption that he won't (or shouldn't), the enemy has us right where he wants us—primed for the spiritual angst that comes whenever we count on promises God never made and ignore realities we don't want to see. It's a dangerous place to be. Just ask Asaph. Or Job's wife. Or Tim.

As we saw earlier, it's no accident that the first story in the Bible after the fall of Adam and Eve is a story of a bad guy killing a good guy and mostly getting away with it.[5] It's as if God is trying to tell us right off the bat that in a fallen world lots of things won't go as we'd hope or expect.

In the same vein, Jesus knew what he was doing when he warned us to count the cost before stepping out to follow him.[6] Sure, the rewards are incredible and the downside of rejecting him terrifying. But in the short run, being on his team is not always what it's cracked up to be. He knew our fickle tendencies. He knew how quickly we accept the good things (and praise him for them) and how quickly we can turn on him when things go wrong (which is what made Job such a rare and righteous man).[7]

Eddie Haskell Christians

This myth of a God who brings good luck does more than just produce devastating spiritual disillusionment—it also produces Eddie Haskell Christianity.

Eddie Haskell was the two-faced, kiss-up best friend of Wally Cleaver in the classic 1950s sitcom *Leave It to Beaver*. In the presence of Wally's parents, he was a solicitous, well-mannered young man. When they weren't around, he was a punk. He was also certain that none of the adults in his life were smart enough to see through his scam.

Over the years I've run across a surprising number of people who look at God a lot like Eddie Haskell looked at Ward and June Cleaver. They think he's stupid. They wouldn't use those words and would be aghast if called out on it. But their actions give them away. They carefully observe a few outward religious rituals while living like hell the rest of the time. It's as if they assume that God can't see or figure out what they do outside of church.

Now, why would anybody play the religious game in public if they don't buy it in private? In the past it was partly due to peer pressure and strong cultural expectations. It was something some people felt they had to do in order to sell insurance or get elected to public office. But those days are pretty much gone.

Today those who play this game do so mostly to cover their spiritual bases. Which explains why the trash-talking basketball player rushes through the sign of the cross before shooting a free throw, why the young soldier keeps a cross around his neck despite the porn in his locker, and why lots of suburban families have a big Bible on the coffee table to keep it from floating away. They all figure that a little bit of God might bring a little bit of luck. So why not rub the bottle and see if a genie pops out?

But when such thinking runs rampant, the results are spiritually disastrous. It creates a form of cultural Christianity filled with rituals, symbols, and rules that everyone abides by but no one believes. Ultimately it plays God for a fool. It's Eddie Haskell Christianity.

And it never works. God is not fooled by such behavior. He's pretty smart at figuring things out. Just ask the Israelites.

They thought their pedigree, circumcision, and sacrifices would be more than enough to convince God to bless them. They were sure it would bring them good luck and victory over their enemies despite their propensity to worship other gods, oppress the downtrodden, and ignore justice. After all, even if they were messing up, they were nowhere near as evil as the surrounding nations. But to their shock, their empty religious rituals brought them neither protection nor victory, though it did eventually earn them an all-expenses-paid trip to Babylon.[8]

The same principles are at work today when some of us assume that getting baptized, going to church, being confirmed, putting money in the till, helping out in Sunday school, or doing any other religious rituals and activities can cover up a closet full of sins or a lukewarm heart. Rather than giving us a little bit of luck in exchange for a little bit of obedience, God is much more likely to do something else—spit us out. Because he'd actually rather have us ice cold than spiritually lukewarm. He said so himself.[9]

So, Why Bother?

If a halfhearted nod to God doesn't do much good (and, in fact, tends to make matters worse), and if the innocence of an Asaph and the righteousness of a Job can't guarantee God's temporal blessings, why bother? (I know that in the end Job got back double what he'd lost. But when you're already the richest guy in the neighborhood, so what? It's not worth the anguish. It's certainly not a trade I'd make if given the choice. Bet you wouldn't either.)

The thing we have to remember is that the benefits of righteousness aren't primarily found in earthly rewards. They're found in the next life. The great benefit is forgiveness. The great reward is heaven. Everything else is merely an hors d'oeuvre, a small appetizer before the great feast.

To measure the glory of the king's table by the finger food (or the absence of finger food) would be silly. Same for measuring God's goodness and rewards by yesterday's fender bender or even today's tragic medical diagnosis.

Those like Asaph who nearly bail out on God, and those like Tim who actually do turn their back and walk away, usually arrive at their point of despair by using some faulty math. When figuring out whether following the Lord is worth the cost, they put the wrong benefits into the equation. They plug in the earthly where the eternal belongs.

> *To measure the glory of the king's table by the finger food (or the absence of finger food) would be silly. Same for measuring God's goodness and rewards by yesterday's fender bender or even today's tragic medical diagnosis.*

The only way to accurately measure God's goodness is to look to the cross. The only way to accurately measure his provision is to look to heaven. Everything else provides a false reading.

Wouldn't It Be Worth It Anyway?

I've heard some people say that following Jesus has brought so much joy and meaning into their life that they would do it again even if they found out the gospel wasn't true.

I have to admit, I've never quite gotten their point. I can't see how or why following a lie would ever be a good thing. My guess is that they're trying to counterbalance what they see as an overemphasis on heavenly rewards (which some mockingly call pie-in-the-sky Christianity) and a corresponding lack of concern for the temporal needs of those who are hurting.

But while their motivation may be right (a desire to ensure that we don't become so heavenly minded that we're no earthly good), their logic is absurd.

If Christ is not raised, our faith is worthless. If he's not a *living* Lord, we're still in our sins. If there is no heaven for those who follow him, we're fools. We haven't chosen an admirable path. We haven't chosen an ethical path. We've chosen an idiot's path.

And no, that's not just my opinion. It's the opinion of none other than the apostle Paul himself. (It's also God's opinion, if we believe the Scriptures are his handiwork.) Paul says that if our hope in Christ is primarily rooted in this life, we are to be most pitied. We've taken the fool's path.[10]

True Words, Wrong Message

Yet I find it interesting that when it comes to sharing our faith, we tend to put almost all the focus on earthly benefits, as if that's the ultimate deal closer.

For instance, in the classic evangelism tool known as the *Four Spiritual Laws,* Law 1 reads, "God loves you and has a wonderful plan for your life." It's followed by John 3:16 and a partial quote of John 10:10 that says, "I am come that they might have life, and that they might have it more abundantly" (KJV).

The problem doesn't lie in the words of the first law or in the two verses used to support it. They're all true. The problem lies in the way that most people interpret those words. The average man or woman on the street hears them and assumes that God's "wonderful plan" for his or her life and Jesus's offer of an "abundant life" refer to a better and more wonderful experience right here on earth.

After all, that's what the term *abundant* usually implies in the English language. It conjures up images of wealth and excess. It's synonymous with plentiful. To most of us, an "abundant life" sounds an awful lot like the "good life."

Yet Jesus's words in John 10:10 don't refer to a life of greater ease, prosperity, and protection from Job-like trials. When looking at the larger context, it's clear that Jesus was talking about salvation. In contrast to the thief who comes to kill and destroy, Jesus comes as a good shepherd, ready and willing to lay down his life so that we might live rather than die at the hands of the enemy. No question, that's excessive, abundant, and beyond all expectations. But it has nothing to do with earthly abundance and success.

Now, don't get me wrong. I have no problem with the *Four Spiritual Laws*. I've used the booklet countless times to help people grasp the gospel message. I even have an autographed copy (by its creator, Bill Bright) in my office. But it seems to me that in our zeal to see people come to Christ, we often paint a picture of a wonderful and abundant Christian life that effectively ignores, downplays, and even negates the harder teachings of Jesus.

While that might speed along so-called decisions for Christ, it does little to prepare a fledgling disciple for what's ahead. In fact, it does the opposite. It sets the stage for disillusionment when things don't turn out so well.

We do non-Christians, new Christians, and even longtime Christians a disservice when we neglect the *many* scriptures that speak of hardship, persecution, and self-sacrifice while focusing on just *one* verse that appears (incorrectly) to promise a life of good luck, ease, and a steady stream of success.[11]

Good News or Bad News?

I want to be clear. I'm not saying that we should go through life looking over our shoulder, pessimistically waiting for the hammer to fall. The fact that God doesn't bring or promise us good luck and earthly success doesn't mean we're all doomed to bad luck and failure.

Christianity is not a religion of gloom. Properly understood, it's a faith filled with hope and joy.[12] The fact is, righteous living often does bring great rewards in this life. As Solomon so forcefully points out in the book of Proverbs, righteousness *generally* brings stellar results. But as we saw in an earlier chapter, his proverbs aren't God's promises. They are God-inspired statements about how life *generally* works. So, while righteous living may *generally* bring stellar results, it doesn't always. There is no guarantee.

And it's precisely for these exceptions (the situations when the eternal rewards of righteousness seem to be the only rewards) that we need to be prepared.

There's no real danger of spiritual disillusionment when things go better than expected. No one rails against God because they've been "blessed too much" in this life. The spiritual danger comes at those times when all the blessings seem to be eternal—and we expected them to start showing up today. It's then that we're prone to think God has let us down or, like Tim, to believe that we've been sold a bill of goods.

That's why unrealistic and unfounded spiritual expectations need to be exposed for what they are: wishful thinking. Truth isn't always what we want to hear or would like to believe. But it is truth. Everything else is a mirage. These mirage-type truths might give us hope for the day. They might spur us to keep on going. But eventually they will come up empty. And when they do, they always make things worse, not better.

Earthquakes and Persecution

I live in a coastal suburb of San Diego. Like most of Southern California, it's in an earthquake zone. While we aren't in a high-risk area, the risk is genuine. Big earthquakes happen. They don't happen here daily or even annually. In fact, in my part of San Diego, we can go a century or two without a big one. But they do happen. And only a fool builds his house as if they don't.

The same goes for the inevitable trials of life and persecutions that come to us as God's people. Some of us live in persecution- and trial-prone areas. Some of us don't. Throughout history there have been times and places where living for Jesus was easy, and there have been times and places where it was life threatening. The same is true today. Following Jesus has very different consequences in San Diego than in Saudi Arabia. The cost was different in 1950 than in the twenty-first century. The accompanying difficulties are far greater in Hollywood or New York than in Bakersfield (California) or Wheaton (Illinois).

To assume or proclaim that following Jesus should make this life easier or better is a huge mistake. To assume that godliness is a means to financial gain is even worse. It's a sign that we've been robbed of the truth and think with a corrupt mind.[13]

It might help recruiting. It might cast a wider net and draw a bigger crowd. But ultimately it's guaranteed to leave those of us who face the tougher trials and greater persecutions wondering what went wrong. It sets the stage for the enemy to whisper his accusations against God's goodness and justice. It sets the stage for us to believe him.

> *When we know the cost and count the cost before the journey begins, we aren't likely to be blown away when it's time to pay the bill.*

Unrealistic expectations never make for solid footing. Be it a marriage, a purchase, a business partner, a vacation, or our walk with God, unfounded and unrealistic expectations are always a recipe for confusion and disillusionment. Sure, some people with unfounded and idealistic expectations find that things went just as they expected. But that doesn't make them wise. It just makes them lucky.

Thinning the Herd

By the way, there's one other benefit of letting people know on the front end that while following God has an incredible eternal reward, the earthly benefits aren't always so great.

It thins the herd.

Eddie Haskell Christians don't pretend to sign up for a faith that is just as likely to bring trials, persecution, and hardship as earthly fortune and success. Perhaps that's why the persecuted church has always been a spiritually strong church. It doesn't attract a lot of pretenders or dabblers.

When we know the cost and count the cost before the journey begins, we aren't likely to be blown away when it's time to pay the bill. But when Jesus's warnings about some difficult terrain along the way are listed in small print or ignored altogether, it's a different matter. When we assume, imply, or promise that God is supposed to bring us good luck and lots of success, we're set up for deep disappointment and spiritual cynicism.

Even worse, we risk turning the King of kings into little more than a good-luck charm. And that's a role he never agreed to play.

DOES GOD BRING GOOD LUCK?

"Skin for skin!" Satan replied. "A man will give all he has for his own life. But stretch out your hand and strike his flesh and bones, and he will surely curse you to your face."

The LORD said to Satan, "Very well, then, he is in your hands; but you must spare his life."

So Satan went out from the presence of the LORD and afflicted Job with painful sores from the soles of his feet to the top of his head. Then Job took a piece of broken pottery and scraped himself with it as he sat among the ashes.

His wife said to him, "Are you still holding on to your integrity? Curse God and die!" He replied, *"You are talking like a foolish woman. Shall we accept good from God, and not trouble?"*

In all this, Job did not sin in what he said.

JOB 2:4–10

9
A VALLEY MEANS A WRONG TURN

My first three years as a pastor were miserable. To this day, my wife and I still affectionately (okay, not so affectionately) call them the Dark Years. I've written about them before, so I won't go into much detail here.[1] But suffice it to say, they were spiritually, professionally, and emotionally crushing. Nothing went right. I was in a three-year funk. Good days were rare. Nights were no better, just another chance to toss, turn, and worry some more.

However, it wasn't the problems we faced that made that particular valley so devastating. Nancy and I have dealt with far worse—her battle with cancer, the betrayal of a trusted ally, the meltdown of our financial savings, not to mention all the typical trials and tragedies that come to anyone with a few miles on their odometer.

What made this particular valley so demoralizing was its timing. It came immediately after (and as a direct result of) a step of obedience. It was as if God asked us to step forward and then slapped us down for doing so.

What we thought would be a place of still waters ended up as a boiling cauldron of conflict. At first I shrugged it off as a temporary trial. No big deal. After all, it's a well-known fact that trials are part of the package when we sign up to follow Christ. But when it began to look like this particular trial had no end in sight…well, let's just say I started to look at things differently.

Two Options

As I tried to figure out what to do next, I was caught between two competing directives. On the one hand, I *knew* what God wanted me to do: stick it out. On the other hand, most of my friends were absolutely certain that they knew what I should do: move on. It was all rather confusing—and frustrating.

The Case for Staying

As far as coming to San Diego to serve as the church's pastor, I had no doubts that God had brought us here. His leading had been quite clear, punctuated by a series of divine "coincidences" that had his fingerprints all over them. But after a couple of frustrating years, and without much indication that anything would ever change, it seemed as if it was time to move on.

Except for one problem: God had also made it clear to me that I was supposed to move into the community, dig deep roots, and stay for the long haul.

Still, the longer things went sideways, the more I began to wonder if I'd misunderstood. Actually, I *hoped* I'd misunderstood. The prospect of sticking around for a lifetime of frustrating ministry with minimal fruit in an environment where success seemed improbable didn't jibe with my idea of God's wonderful plan for my life.

The Case for Leaving

Lots of my friends and mentors felt the same way. They couldn't imagine God calling me to serve in an unreceptive environment and then asking me to stay. (I guess they'd forgotten about Jeremiah.) So every time another opportunity came along, they encouraged me to go for it. If I balked and brought up what God had previously told me to do, they assured me I must have gotten it wrong.

I have to admit, there were plenty of days when their advice rang true. After all, it was what I wanted to hear, what I wanted to believe, and what I wanted to do.

What Does a Valley Mean?

Unfortunately my friends' advice was based on a faulty premise. They were convinced that a long-term valley could never be a part of God's long-term plan.

I'm not talking here about the kinds of valleys and trials that are completely out of our control—the medical issues, tragedies, and injustices that we can do nothing about except suck it up, trust God, and endure. I'm talking about the kinds of valleys we can avoid or wiggle out of if we so choose.

From my friends' perspective, only a fool would stay in that kind of valley. They assumed that God's leading always takes us to the mountaintop. They realized there would be an occasional hardship along the way. But they believed it would always be incidental, a short but necessary part of the process. Faced with a lingering valley, especially one with no apparent end in sight, they automatically assumed it meant a wrong turn. They were sure it should be gotten out of as soon as possible, no matter what it took to do so.

Now, obviously, some valleys are the result of a wrong turn. Both the Old and the New Testaments warn of the consequences that come from our sinful and foolish decisions.[2] But the idea that every long-term valley is a mistake and should automatically be wiggled out of is a fallacy. It's based on a spiritual urban legend that can't stand up to scrutiny: the belief that God only leads us to the mountaintop and that long-term valleys always mean a wrong turn. It ignores the long history of God's dealings with his people and the clear teaching of Scripture.[3]

Those who buy into this myth and live by it end up paying a high price. Important spiritual lessons go wanting. Godly character is stunted.

The myth excuses and even encourages self-centered decisions in the name of getting out of the pain as quickly as possible. It even truncates God's power. If we run from every messy situation on the assumption that God can't be in it, we'll never experience the miraculous power of his deliverance. After all, a miracle needs a mess. Always has. Always will. It's part of the equation. Tough trials and help-me-Jesus experiences aren't always a lot of fun. But without them, there's not much need for God to show up.

It's also a belief that hurts others. If we assume that long-term pain and hardship are totally unacceptable and automatically outside God's will, then whatever harm or heartbreak we may cause others in our haste to get out becomes mere collateral damage—an unfortunate but unavoidable part of our quest for happiness.

Think of the guilt-free ease with which our culture breaks promises. Disappointing family, friends, or business associates is no big deal if a commitment we made ends up being far costlier than we had imagined. We assume that everyone will understand. After all, we didn't know what we were getting into. And if they don't understand…well, we've gotta do what we've gotta do. So we break our word—or hire a good lawyer to find us a technicality that will let us out.[4]

Consider the countless marriage vows broken on the assumption that staying in an unhappy or unfulfilling marriage can't be God's will. "For better or worse" has somehow become "Until I can't take it anymore." So when things get tough, we move on, convinced that God will understand—and approve.

Here's the kicker.

Most of us understand that hardships (even long-term hardships) are a natural part of life. We know theoretically that God uses them to train and equip us, to build character, and to sometimes carry out his will. That's Christianity 101.

But something fundamentally changes when the deep and lengthy valley is *our* valley. The truths we so easily accept in theory and so quickly apply to others become difficult to fathom in our own life.

Let's admit it: it's pretty hard to imagine any scenario in which an all-knowing and all-loving God would want *us* to endure a lengthy season of frustration and disappointment. That's why, when we find ourselves (or those we love) mired in an extended painful valley, we tend to immediately start looking for the quickest way out. We assume something must have gone terribly wrong.

I wish I could say it's a trap I've never fallen into. But that would be a lie. The myth that a valley must mean a wrong turn tends to gain credibility the longer or deeper our own personal valley gets.

That's what left me so conflicted during my Dark Years. In my head I knew exactly what God wanted me to do: stick it out. But the longer it looked like things might not ever change, the harder it was to accept an answer I didn't want to hear.

So, What Does a Valley Mean?

If a valley doesn't necessarily mean a wrong turn, then what does it mean?

It all depends.

Valleys come in all shapes and sizes. Some have an obvious end in sight; others look like they'll last forever. Some are self-induced; some are merely the result of living in a fallen world; some are obviously God's will; and some are nearly impossible to figure out until we're safely on the other side.

But no matter what kind of valley we face, there are certain things we need to know in order to think clearly and respond properly. It doesn't matter if it's a self-induced, wrong turn, an *I goofed up big time* valley, or a valley of God's choosing; here's what we need to ask ourselves:

- *Why am I here?*
- *How should I respond?*
- *What can I learn?*

I've found these three simple but profound fog-cutting questions to be incredibly helpful. They've repeatedly enabled me and those I've worked with to navigate life's deeper valleys in a way that honors God, doesn't short-circuit spiritual growth, and still allows us to get out of the valley as soon as it's appropriate. So let's look at each one more closely.

Why Am I Here?

The problem with assuming that every deep and extended valley must mean a wrong turn is that it ignores so much biblical evidence to the contrary. Sometimes a valley does mean a wrong turn, but just as often (if not more often) it means something altogether different.

Did God Send Me Here?

Some valleys are *God sent me here* valleys. Their distinguishing trait is obedience that appears to have backfired. Whenever doing the right thing is what puts us into a valley or keeps us there, it's a good bet that we're right where God wants us to be, even though we'd almost always rather be somewhere else.

For instance, when God sent Jacob's family into Egypt to live with Joseph, it was the beginning of a *God sent me here* valley that would last for centuries. At the time, they thought they were moving to Egypt for the easy life. Though God had previously told Abraham exactly what would happen, Jacob, Joseph, and his brothers had no idea that the Egyptian leaders would eventually turn on them or that their descendants would be forced to endure harsh slavery while God enlarged their numbers and prepared them for nationhood. Had they known that, my guess is that they would have opted out. But it was all part of God's plan. It was a valley of his choosing.[5]

Then, as soon as they got out of Egypt, God sent them right back into another *God sent me here* valley. He told them to set up camp at the worst possible site. They were surrounded by two mountains, an impassible body of water, and an advancing army of far superior strength.

You probably know the rest of the story. At the last moment

God stepped in. He parted the Red Sea, told the Israelites to walk to the other side, and let the Egyptians all take a bath. Because we know how things ended up, the valley doesn't look so bad. In fact, for some of us it looks like an exciting *wish I was there* adventure. But the Israelites had no idea what God was up to. They weren't reading a great Sunday-school story. They were living a scary reality—a terrifying reality. Yet they were also right where God wanted them to be.[6]

Jesus himself went through a number of *God sent me here* valleys. The first one came immediately after his baptism. The Holy Spirit sent him into the wilderness to fast and wait for further instructions. After he had reached a point of great physical weakness, the devil showed up ready for battle. It was hardly the ideal time to face a tough and genuine temptation from the great tempter himself. Yet it was all part of the Father's plan. It was no mistake. No one had made a wrong turn.[7]

Later, Jesus ran his disciples through a similar drill. One day he told them to get into a boat and head to the other side of the lake. About halfway across, they encountered a sudden, life-threatening squall.

They panicked.

He slept.

Well, actually, he slept until they woke him up. Then he told the storm to shut up. After that (knowing Jesus), he probably went back to sleep. For the disciples, it was a horrifying experience. For Jesus, it was just another lesson the boys had to learn.[8]

From Joseph's descendants to Jesus's disciples, all these trials and valleys share one thing in common. They were the direct result of doing exactly what God said to do. They were *God sent me here* valleys. Fortunately, there is one thing we can know for sure when obeying God puts us in deep weeds: we're right where he wants us to be, even if we aren't where we want to be. That may not make the valley any less scary or wearisome, but it does provide a source of spiritual comfort and perspective.

Did I Mess Up?

A second kind of valley is found in the self-induced darkness that follows a rebellious or foolish decision. It's the one valley that does mean someone took a wrong turn somewhere along the line. It's the high price of living life as a self-guided tour.

An example would be the Israelites' cycles of subjugation to the Canaanites, Philistines, Babylonians, and Assyrians. Unlike their period of slavery in Egypt, these times of foreign domination were never an original part of God's plan. They were self-induced hardships, the direct result of ignoring and disobeying God's law.

The same goes for most of the valleys in King David's life. Except for the time he spent running from a jealous King Saul after David's victory over Goliath, almost all the other valleys he faced were of the *I messed up* variety. Most could be traced back to one dreadful wrong turn: his tryst with Bathsheba and the subsequent murder of her husband. That propelled him on a path filled with broken dreams, political conflicts, and a family in disarray. The dysfunction, incest, murder, and coup d'état that followed were the sad consequence of a side trail he decided to take on his own one night.[9]

One good thing about an *I messed up* valley is that it's almost always easy to find the connection between the wrong turn and the valley. There's no subtlety. God doesn't hide what's happening. When we make a willful decision (or a series of decisions) to stray from the prescribed path, we know it. And even if we make a wrong turn in ignorance, God will eventually make it known to us. He's not out to stump us or mess with our mind. He wants us to know where we went wrong; it's the only way we'll ever get back on track.

Is This Beyond My Understanding?

There is a third type of valley. It's the valley or trial that makes no sense at all. It's what I like to call a *Who knows why?* valley. It has no apparent connection to any step of obedience or step of disobedience. It's just there. Sometimes it can be figured out when viewed through the rearview mirror, but just as often it never makes any sense at all.

Think of Job's sudden run of bad luck. Everyone tried to figure out the reasons. But it was an exercise in futility. His friends didn't get it. His wife didn't get it. Job himself didn't get it. Even when God showed up at the end, he never told anyone why it all happened. The only reason we know what was going on is because we're told at the beginning of the book that bears Job's name. But there's no indication that anyone told Job. And frankly, for most of us who read the explanation, it still doesn't make a lot of sense. It seems out of character for God to be debating with Satan and using Job to prove a point.[10]

Or I think of the early days of Israel's occupation of the Promised Land when a strange thing took place. The men of Judah took possession of the hill country because the Lord was with them. But they were unable to drive out the people who lived in the plains, *because they had iron chariots.*[11]

What?

The Lord was with the men of Judah but they couldn't drive out a bunch of guys who had superior equipment? What's up with that? If I was picking teams on the elementary school playground, I know I'd always pick God over the kid with a couple of iron chariots.

Wouldn't you? I'd also expect to win, big time. But obviously that's not what happened in Judah's case. And we're never told why—except for the fact that the bad guys had some iron chariots.

Clearly that was a *Who knows why?* valley. It's a place that even God's best can find themselves in. Job was God's main man, his pride and joy. The Lord was with the men of Judah. But for some reason the guys with the iron chariots can sometimes kick our butts. Someday I want to ask God why.

How Should I Respond?

Once we know what kind of valley we're in (even if it's a valley that makes no sense), it's time to answer the second question: *How should I respond?* It's a question best left unanswered until we know what kind of valley we are in, because different kinds of valleys call for different kinds of responses. But once we have a clear idea why, it's not too hard to figure out what to do next.

When to Hang Tough

For instance, *God sent me here* valleys always call for hanging tough. Wiggling out or running away is never a good option. That's a lesson Jonah learned the hard way when he tried to avoid a dreaded assignment. It's a lesson we can learn from Abraham's choice to take the pathway of deception in order to save his own neck. When he claimed Sarah was his sister, all he did was disgrace himself and set in motion a pattern of deception that would eventually tear his family apart when both his son and his grandson used the same ploy to get out of their own sticky situations.[12]

Then there's Daniel. He's the poster child for hanging tough and doing the right thing no matter what. All he had to do to avoid the horrifying prospect of being eaten alive by lions was to stop publicly praying to God for thirty days. Thirty days. Not forever. Just thirty days.[13]

But he wouldn't go there. He knew that a path called disobedience was far worse than a valley called death. So he kept praying and ended up in a lion's den.

Suppose he'd looked at his scary prospects from a different perspective. Suppose he'd believed that a loving and good God would never send him into a terrible valley or ask him to die as a martyr. Suppose he'd assumed that a valley like that surely meant a wrong turn.

He would have responded quite differently. He might have fled. He might have taken a brief spiritual time-out or simply started praying in private. That was a compromise he could have easily justified in light of all the good he would be able to accomplish in his new role as the nation's chief administrator. After all, he certainly wouldn't be much good to God or his people stuck in the bowels of a lion.

> *Never judge the appropriateness of obedience by the short-term or even lifelong results. Judge it by eternity.*

On a much smaller scale—okay, a much, *much* smaller scale—that's what I was facing during my Dark Years. The only way out of what appeared to be a long-term valley was to disobey God's previous instructions.

Fortunately I didn't. But looking back, I shudder to think what would have happened if I'd followed my heart instead of my head. If I'd bought the lie that extended valleys mean a wrong turn, I would have bailed out. I would have missed what has proved to be God's plan for my life and ministry. I would have played out a fallback role on a stage not of his choosing.

Even if obeying God's clear leading is what puts us in a bind or keeps us in a bind, continuing to obey is still the only thing to do, even if it seems to make things worse. Never judge the appropriateness of obedience by the short-term or even lifelong results. Judge it by eternity. Had my Dark Years turned into Dark Decades, staying put still would have been the right thing to do. Had Daniel been eaten by the lions, he still would have made the right move (though, admittedly, we probably wouldn't be telling his story to the kids in Sunday school).

When to Change Direction

While *God sent me here* valleys call for staying put, *I messed up* valleys call for a completely different response. They call for a serious change in direction. If a wrong turn got us there, it usually takes some major retracing of our steps to get us back where we need to be.

Unfortunately, sometimes the consequences of a wrong turn can last a lifetime. That's what happened to my friend Tony. Stuck in jail for a horrendous decision and crime, he came to his senses and turned his life over to God and began to make some serious changes.

But that didn't spring him from prison. He remained incarcerated, with little chance of getting out. What did change, however, were the resources he had available. He found new strength, comfort, and purpose in the midst of the long and monotonous valley he'd put himself into. God began to use him to lead other prisoners to Christ, to teach them the Bible, and to shed light in a very dark place.

Thankfully, most *I messed up* valleys don't last a lifetime. But they are almost always impossible to get out of until we do two things: (1) take personal responsibility, and (2) make some serious changes.

It's obviously foolish to blame God if we find ourselves in a mess that's directly related to ignoring him. But taking responsibility is only the first step. To get out of an *I messed up* valley, we also have to turn around and start heading in a different direction.

It's not enough to just feel sorry for what we've done. We have to actually start doing things differently. Otherwise all we have is good intentions.

We can learn a lot about getting out of an *I messed up* valley from a story found in the book of Judges. For years the Israelites had been crushed by the Ammonites (one of the many "ites" that gave them grief over the years—the Hittites, Amalekites, Moabites, Maonites, Parasites, and Termites).

They found themselves under the thumb of the Ammonites because they had rejected God and started worshiping the false and demonic gods of the surrounding nations. So God did exactly what he'd told them he would do. He sold them into the hands of their enemies. Now, eighteen years later, they suddenly came to their senses and began to cry out to God.

Yet his answer was hardly what we'd expect. The Lord didn't say, "Cool. I'm so glad you've come clean. Now move out of the way while I wipe out your enemies."

No, instead he told them, "I'm tired of it all. I've already delivered you too many times. If you want help, turn to the gods you've already chosen. See what they can do."[14]

Wow! Not exactly the response most of us would expect—or the Israelites expected. Where's the mercy and grace in that? It's rather un-Godlike, except perhaps for the fact that it was God who said it.

So, next, they tried groveling. "We have sinned. Do with us whatever you think best, but please rescue us now."[15]

But still God remained distant.

Finally they got rid of their foreign gods. Only then did God decide to heed their call for help.[16]

The same holds true for us. I've seen lots of people who were sorry for the mess they created, and wished it was different, but were still not willing to change the behaviors that got them into hot water in the first place. The irony is that, for many of them, the longer they stayed in their self-created valley, the angrier at God they became, not realizing that *I messed up* valleys never get better as long as we blame others (or God) and keep messing up.

One more thing about *I messed up* valleys: they don't go away the moment we start heading in the right direction. They often take a long time to get out of—sometimes far longer than they took to get into.

It reminds me of the times I've visited the Grand Canyon. From the rim, it's a short and enticing walk to the lookouts below. But once I decide to turn around and head back out, it's always a lot longer and a lot harder to get back to the top than it was to get down to the lookout.

Or put another way, getting out of a self-inflicted valley is a lot like running a distance race and taking a fall. Once you get back up, it takes some time to catch up. In fact, you have to run harder and faster than everyone else just to get there. After a while, that can start to feel unfair. But that's how it works. There's no way around it—which is why it's a good idea to try not to fall in the first place.

When to Refuse a Shortcut

No matter what kind of valley we're in, there is one thing we can count on: the enemy is sure to offer us a shortcut out.

That's what he offered Jesus when he suggested turning the nearby rocks into bread. After all, it looked like the only way Jesus could survive. He'd already waited on the Father for forty days. Wasn't that enough?

That's also what he offers us when a lie looks like the only way out of a dicey predicament. Or when moral purity looks like the death knell of a longed-for relationship. Or when returning evil for evil seems like the only way to keep from being run over.

> *There are always two ways out of every trial: the enemy's shortcut, which always involves compromise or disobedience, and the way of escape God promises to all who walk with him.*

In each case we already know what we *should* do. The problem occurs when the right path looks like it's taking us to the wrong place or at least to a place where we don't want to go. That's when the enemy's detour starts to look awfully inviting.

The key to successfully resisting is to determine ahead of time that we won't take one of his shortcuts no matter how inviting it looks. To wait until we're at the crossroads to make up our mind is to fight a losing battle with temptation. The path of sin and compromise is just too alluring. Besides that, the enemy's plan often does work. It can take us out of the valley. But even when it does so, it's a lot like quenching our thirst with saltwater. For a moment it sure beats dehydration, but in the long run it only makes matters worse by accelerating our dehydration.

Fact is, there are always two ways out of every trial: the enemy's shortcut, which always involves compromise or disobedience, and the way of escape God promises to all who walk with him.[17] The enemy's shortcuts usually work well in the short run. But they never work well in eternity. The Lord's way of escape (a pathway called faith and obedience) sometimes works well in the short run. But it always shines bright in the light of eternity.[18]

What Can I Learn?

There is one more question besides, *Why am I here?* and, *How should I respond?* It's, *What can I learn?*

There are always lessons to be learned and character to be built no matter what the cause or what the valley. A valley of injustice helps us identify with the sufferings of our Lord. A valley of pain prepares us to empathize and support others who face the same. A valley of suffering teaches obedience and trust. Even a valley of self-induced hardship can serve as a warning to never go there again.

That's why, when writing to a group of spiritual refugees, James told them to rejoice anyway. He knew that their trials had the potential to teach them lessons they could never learn elsewhere. Interestingly, he never addressed the question of whether their persecution was the result of God's doing, the enemy's doing, or just part of life in a fallen world. Instead, he dialed in on the one thing they could benefit from no matter what: the spiritual lessons of perseverance, character, and maturity.[19]

> *If God asked his only begotten Son to go through the valley of the cross, we shouldn't be too surprised when he asks us as his adopted sons and daughters to go through a few valleys of our own.*

In addition, he also encouraged them to ask for wisdom in order to discern how they should respond and what they should learn. During my Dark Years, that prayer became a favorite of mine. I found that as I asked for insight into what I could learn, rather than constantly looking for ways to get out, the life lessons opened up on a steady basis. In fact, looking back, I now realize that most of the leadership and spiritual lessons I teach and write about had their genesis during a season of life when I thought nothing good was happening.

That's not to say that every trial and valley is a good thing. That's not to pin every tragedy on God. That's not to say that valleys are any fun (if you like it when things fall apart, you're weird—or a repairman). But it is to say that, as long as we have to go through it, we might as well get something out of it.

If God asked his only begotten Son to go through the valley of the cross, we shouldn't be too surprised when he asks us as his adopted sons and daughters to go through a few valleys of our own. If Jesus learned obedience through the things he suffered, we shouldn't be surprised if we're asked to take the same course.[20]

DOES A VALLEY MEAN A WRONG TURN?

The LORD said to Moses, "Tell the Israelites to turn back and encamp near Pi Hahiroth, between Migdol and the sea. They are to encamp by the sea, directly opposite Baal Zephon. Pharaoh will think, 'The Israelites are wandering around the land in confusion, hemmed in by the desert.' And I will harden Pharaoh's heart, and he will pursue them. But I will gain glory for myself through Pharaoh and all his army, and the Egyptians will know that I am the LORD."

EXODUS 14:1–4

10 DEAD PEOPLE GO TO A BETTER PLACE

Would you like to see a mini riot up close? Here's what you do. The next time you're at a funeral, stand up and tell the truth, the whole truth, and nothing but the truth about the dearly departed. Then step back to see what happens.

It should be interesting.

When it comes to funerals and memorial services, we have deep-seated, unwritten rules—cultural norms that are ignored at great social peril. Funerals call for praise and fond memories. They put things in the best possible light. It's not the time for critique or brutal honesty. It's the time to remember the best moments in the life of the one we've lost, even if some of us are pretty happy to be rid of the scoundrel.

Now, don't get me wrong, I don't have a problem with that. I get it that bereaved family and friends need comfort, not a bucket of cold water. I realize that every life bears the image of God, even when it has been badly marred. I'm more than happy to sit through a service where weird Uncle Tom is described as "inquisitive and fun-loving" or hotheaded Suzy is described as "feisty and passionate." I don't even mind when mean, old Mr. Warren is labeled as caring and sensitive by those who "really knew him."

But there is one step that is a step too far. It's the point at which I cringe and bite my lip if I'm in the crowd. It's the point at which I refuse to participate if I'm the guy up front officiating. It's when wicked Uncle Ernie is described as being in a better place.

He's not.

Funeral Assurances

Jesus and the Bible are quite clear—the wicked don't go to a better place. There's a real hell. It's not the devil's playground. It's not a perpetual wild party. It's Satan's worst nightmare.[1]

Yet as any pastor who has ever officiated at a memorial service knows, the social pressure to offer funeral assurances, even for wicked Uncle Ernie, is incredibly strong. At the point of death, lots of us believe (and want to be assured) that the recently departed has gone to a better place no matter what.

> *There's a real hell. It's not the devil's playground. It's not a perpetual wild party. It's Satan's worst nightmare.*

But it's a myth—another popular but completely unfounded spiritual urban legend. Dead people don't always go to a better place. That might be what we'd like to believe. It has a nice ring to it. But it's not true.

And it's not just wicked Uncle Ernie who misses out. The same goes for the sweet lady next door who would never hurt a fly but would also never bow the knee to Jesus. Or the morally upright cousin who just happened to also be a card-carrying member of a cult claiming that Jesus and Satan were brothers and God was once a man. Or the sincere Buddhist coworker who graciously and heroically battled cancer without a trace of bitterness thanks to his deep trust in the tenets of his faith.

If the words of Jesus and the teachings of the New Testament mean what they say, these wonderful people and friends aren't in a better place either. We might wish they were. But they're not.

This is not something I write with glee. I pen it with a heavy heart. If I were in charge of the universe, it would be different. But I'm not. And by now I've learned that whenever God and I disagree over how to run things, he's always right.

I guess that's why we call him God.

Wishful Thinking

To our modern-day sensibilities, the exclusivity of Christ, the reality of hell, and the need for a salvation that includes personal piety have all become passé, if not downright offensive. And it's not just our culture that rejects these ideas; so do many Christians.

The widespread denial of any sort of actual judgment or a place called hell is nowhere more evident than when we deal with death. It's here that it becomes obvious that funeral assurances are much more than a social custom. For many if not most folks, they're a deeply held, core belief.

If you don't think so, try questioning the eternal destiny of someone who recently passed away. See how many looks of disgust you get. See if you can avoid a fistfight. And, no, I don't mean do it at the funeral service. I don't mean bring it up to family or close friends. I mean you should give it a shot a couple of weeks later in a casual conversation as you're having a latte with a mutual friend.

It will be interesting—I guarantee you.

There are numerous ways we go about justifying that nearly everyone we know ends up in a better place when they die. The justifications change depending on how close we were to the person and what we knew about them.

For instance, if they were genuinely following Christ, it's easy. Jesus said they'd go to heaven. Who are we to argue?

But for those who clearly didn't follow Christ, we tend to use different standards. The first thing we look for is any evidence of a brief nod to God somewhere in the past. It doesn't matter how casual, short-lived, or spiritually fruitless it might have been. If we can find one, that's enough to give many of us all the confidence we need to know that they are now safely in the presence of the Lord.

> *Finding peace or offering someone encouragement based on a nod to God, sincerity, or a good heart belied by bad actions is a lot like a doctor telling the star quarterback that he'll be able to play in next Friday's game—despite the x-ray he holds in his hand revealing a badly broken leg.*

If we can't find evidence of a fleeting Jesus moment, we turn to another standard: virtue. A life of basic morality, especially one coupled with a sincere belief in another religious value system, is all that many of us need to be certain that our friend or loved one is now in a better place.

Even if we can't find much morality or sincerity, there's still one more card to play. It's the "good heart" card. As in "I know he had a good heart. He meant well. He just got sucked into the wrong crowd." It's the card we play when all the evidence points elsewhere.

But try as we might to find comfort and assurance in such rationalizations and mental gymnastics, the comfort we feel is bogus. It's totally at odds with Scripture. Finding peace or offering someone encouragement based on a nod to God, sincerity, or a good heart belied by bad actions is a lot like a doctor telling the star quarterback that he'll be able to play in next Friday's game—despite the x-ray he holds in his hand revealing a badly broken leg. It might make everyone feel a lot better. Temporarily. But come next Friday, the only football game that young man will be playing is on a video screen.

Eternal destiny isn't determined by where we wish people would go. It's not determined by where everyone says they went. It's determined by where God puts us (or more precisely, by where we put ourselves).

Don't Blame Me; Blame Jesus

If all this sounds harsh or narrow-minded, don't blame me. Blame Jesus. He's the One who said the path was narrow and few would enter in. It's not as if he danced around the issue. He spoke of it often.[2]

I find it interesting that some scholars try to explain away the more uncomfortable parts of Jesus's teachings about heaven and hell as an accommodation to the beliefs and religious conventions of his day. But that hardly fits with the Jesus we read about in the New Testament. He was anything but accommodating. He was an equal opportunity offender. He skewered everybody's sacred cows, from the man on the street to the theologians and religious leaders.

Think of the time he instigated a lengthy one-on-one chat with a promiscuous Samaritan woman. Or his choice of a hated tax collector named Matthew to be in his inner circle. Or repeatedly violating the Sabbath traditions, hanging out with sinners, and allowing a prostitute to publicly wash his feet with her hair and tears.[3] That's not the stuff of accommodation.

All of these examples make it hard to believe that he was suddenly playing along with the prejudices and fears of his day when he spoke of heaven actually having entrance requirements. It just doesn't fit.

Furthermore, Jesus clearly didn't downplay the fear of hell. He did the opposite. He told his followers to worry about the one who could cast them into hell. He bluntly warned the Pharisees and religious scholars that when they died, there was no way they'd be waking up in a better place. And, of course, he famously asserted that he was the *only* way to get to the Father and heaven—something the apostles and New Testament are just as adamant about.[4]

So unless Jesus and his apostles were somehow wrong about this whole judgment and eternity thing (which would be a strange idea for a Christian to assert), there's no reason to believe that those who don't follow Jesus somehow still end up in a better place anyway.

According to Jesus and the New Testament, they don't.

The Myth Behind the Myth

The idea that dead people always go to a better place actually flows out of another myth. But it's a myth different from most of the spiritual urban legends we've looked at, because though widely held, it's seldom publicly acknowledged, especially by Christians who have been around the block a few times and want to keep their reputation as a Bible-believing Christian. It's the belief-that-shall-not-be-named:

the conviction that all roads eventually lead to the same place despite what Jesus may have said.

Most biblically literate Christians know that such thinking doesn't fit with the words of Jesus and the Bible. But when push comes to shove, when it comes to the eternal destiny of real people we know and love, a large number of us choose to create our own theology, to believe what we want to believe. And that helps explain why no one ever objects when the preacher assures us that the dead guy (whoever he is and whatever he's done) is now in a better place.

Sometimes We Hear What We Want to Hear

The belief that all roads lead to the same place is not only more widely held than many Christian leaders realize; it's also more deeply ingrained. In many cases it doesn't matter what is proclaimed from the pulpit or what the official stance of a church or denomination may be. We believe what we want to believe. We hear what we want to hear.

The fact is, the more our world becomes a global village, and the more our nation becomes culturally diverse, the more many of us want to include everyone as a spiritual family member—even those who are unwilling to acknowledge our Father as *the* Father.

That's what was behind an e-mail I received a couple of years ago from a parent who was appalled at what his daughter had been taught in our junior-high ministry. It went something like this:

My daughter came home from church Sunday morning very upset. She felt her teacher was bad-mouthing other religions and saying people who follow other religions are wrong and not acceptable to God.

We have taught our children to be Christian, which means

accepting all others rather than judging. Who makes us better than someone else? There is no roped-off line at the entrance to heaven for only certain religions.

My daughter said it made her feel very uncomfortable. I'm sure you realize that something like this can really hurt a young person's beliefs.

Please look into what is being taught to our young people. It should not be based on the opinion of their teachers. It should be Christian.

The fact that this e-mail came from a man who regularly attended our services—taking notes and claiming to get a lot out of the messages—could be taken as an indictment of our teaching. But I don't think so. I went back and looked up the messages right around the time of his e-mail. They included at least two sermons that directly contradicted everything he espoused. They weren't obscure. They weren't subtle. They didn't mince words.

The problem wasn't in what he was taught.

The problem was in how he listened.

Like many people who have their mind already made up, when presented with a truth he didn't like, he tuned it out. It reminds me of a group of hearing-impaired students at a school my dad once worked at. When they didn't like what the teacher was saying, they turned down their hearing aids. In essence, that's what this father had done. As a result, it was as if he'd never heard a word we said.

That also explains why his e-mail wasn't a personal rebuke or a challenge to our church's position. Even though he'd heard the words we teach on numerous times, they simply didn't register. He assumed I would be just as upset as he was and would back him up. He fully expected me to take our junior-high staff to the woodshed.

Why This Is So Important

Why is this so important? Why not leave such an uncomfortable and politically incorrect discussion for another time or place? After all, the concept of heaven and hell is an admittedly messy subject.

The reason is simple. The cross and salvation are central to the gospel. Once we lose any real concept of hell, the natural consequence is more than just putting us at odds with Scripture; it eventually devalues the cross, redefines salvation, and turns obedience into an extra-credit spiritual add-on.

Like all the rest of the myths and spiritual urban legends we've looked at, the belief that all dead people go to a better place is not just an error of fact. It's an error that inevitably leads to harmful spiritual results; in this case, not only for those who buy into it, but also for those who never hear about Jesus because of it.

Whatever Happened to Evangelism?

One of the worst side effects is what this myth does to evangelism. It kills any sense of urgency. That not only hurts us as individuals (because we end up failing to do what Jesus told us to do); it also hurts those we were supposed to tell about him.

Urgency

Early church believers felt so passionate about the need to evangelize that they were willing to die trying. Today many of us see things differently. Evangelism is not only no longer worth dying for; it's hardly worth stressing a relationship over. The biggest roadblock to sharing our faith is no longer the loss of our lives, our jobs, or our families. It's the fear of embarrassment. That's enough to keep many of us quiet. We don't want to look dumb; we don't want to be rejected.

How strong is this loss of urgency? I'm told by those who study such things that up to 50 percent of our churches fail to win even one convert to Christ per year. On the one hand, that's hard to square with Jesus's command to go into all the world and make disciples.[5] But on the other hand, it makes perfect sense if many of us believe everyone is going to heaven anyway. In that case, why risk being embarrassed, misunderstood, or ostracized?

Arrogance

But the myth that all dead people go to a better place not only removes any urgency to share Christ; it also makes the very idea of evangelism seem like an arrogant imposition. After all, if all paths work, what makes our path any better than the others?

That was the thinking behind the irate e-mail I received. The young girl's father assumed that Mormons, Jehovah Witnesses, and Muslims all had perfectly adequate paths to salvation. So when the differences between these three faiths and historic Christianity were pointed out in a junior-high Sunday-school class, he found it offensive. He couldn't understand why we would want to challenge the beliefs of people who were already happy with the path they were on.

Priorities

This myth undercuts evangelism in still another way. It relegates the need for salvation to the back of the line. Once we decide that following Christ is merely the best path, but not the only path, then it's not long until we decide that our neighbors, community, and world have far more pressing needs to address than coming to know Jesus.

If eternity is already taken care of for pretty much everybody, why focus our limited time, energy, and money on trying to convert people? Instead, genuine compassion would call for dealing with the immediate, immense, and pressing needs all around us—the stuff of the here and now.

> *Once we lose any real concept of hell, the natural consequence is more than just putting us at odds with Scripture; it eventually devalues the cross, redefines salvation, and turns obedience into an extra-credit spiritual add-on.*

I'm not saying that these things are unimportant. They're incredibly important. Caring for the poor is a sign of the kingdom and a telling trait of righteousness. It's the wicked who don't give a rip. And justice, mercy, and humility are required of us all.[6]

But Jesus also said, "What good is it for a man to gain the whole world, yet forfeit his soul?"[7]

When conversion becomes unnecessary (just an opportunity to share a better way, rather than the only way to God), then digging wells, eradicating disease, and protecting the environment obviously take precedence. And in many cases, it's not long until compassion and liberation are no longer viewed as the essential other side of the evangelism coin; they become the only side of the coin that matters.

How Did Obedience Become Extra Credit?

It's not only evangelistic zeal and fervor that this myth kills off. It also undercuts obedience. When a nod to God is all it takes to be right with God, everything else becomes extra credit.

I don't mean to imply that we have to somehow earn our salvation.

That can't be done. God doesn't grade on a curve. We can never do enough good things to pay off the debt of our sins. Otherwise there would have been no reason for Jesus to die on the cross.[8]

But at the same time, the presumption that we can live like hell and still be confident of ending up in heaven is an idea that Jesus and the authors of the New Testament would find quite odd.

A Young Seeker

Compare the way that Jesus dealt with a young man who wanted to know how to inherit eternal life with the way that many of us would handle the same situation today. Jesus didn't give him a prayer to pray. He didn't ask him if he was ready and willing to accept him as Savior. Instead, he gave him a command—and then stepped back to see if he would do it.[9]

When the young man was unwilling, Jesus didn't say, "Hey, that's okay. I understand. At least we've got your eternal life squared away. I hope someday you'll be ready to come back and follow."

No, he let the young man go and then immediately turned to his followers and told them a story illustrating how hard it is to get into heaven.

Now put the same young man in a time machine and let him show up asking some of us how to inherit eternal life. My bet is that many of us would lead him in a prayer and then give him a follow-up packet filled with information designed to assure him of his salvation and filled with suggestions for some things he might want to do in order to grow in his newfound faith.

A Christian Gangster?

In his book *Loving God*, Chuck Colson tells the story of a Hollywood gangster named Mickey Cohen. Apparently Mickey attended a Billy Graham crusade and afterward decided to "accept Christ." Later, when informed by Graham's associates that as a new Christian he needed to cut his mob ties, Mickey was incredulous.

"You never told me that I had to give up my career. You never told me that I had to give up my friends. There are Christian movie stars, Christian athletes, Christian businessmen. So what's the matter with being a Christian gangster? If I have to give up all that—if that's Christianity—count me out."[10]

Admittedly, Cohen's response was rather extreme. I've not met many people who think God would be cool with Christian gangster as a career choice. Bet you haven't either. But I also bet that you know more than a few folks who think they can be right with God while ignoring most everything he tells them to do. Like Cohen, they've relegated obedience to the status of an extra-credit assignment for those who are really into this Jesus thing.

Setting Up Camp

The Bible is full of stories of people who knew God and yet did some pretty hellish things. We find comfort there, because many of us have found ourselves in a place far from God after having come to know him. That's probably why the story of the prodigal son is such a favorite. Lots of us have been there.[11]

Certainly good and godly people can *fall* into sin (either suddenly or as the result of a series of steps in the wrong direction). And without a doubt, all of us *struggle with sin*. Even the writers of Scripture did so.[12]

But *setting up camp* in the land of disobedience and then staying there and defending it as being no big deal? Well, that, according to the Bible, is a different matter. That's not something real Christians do. The apostle John put it this way: "The man who says, 'I know him,' but does not do what he commands is a liar, and the truth is not in him."[13]

Ouch!

That's pretty harsh. Not much of a funeral assurance there.

Yet it's hardly an obscure Scripture. It's not one of those tough passages we can explain away or brush aside with a few countering verses. The apostle Paul said much the same thing when he warned us against being deceived (his word, not mine) into believing that those who persist in a pattern of willful disobedience will enter the kingdom of heaven anyway.[14] Warnings like these lead me to believe that the early church (at least the churches in Corinth and Galatia) must have also had a good number of folks who were living in high-handed disobedience or who assumed that dead people went to a better place no matter what.

Otherwise, why the warning? These warnings also need to be taken to heart by us today. They don't just undercut the myth that dead people go to a better place no matter how they lived—they should also give us pause if we find ourselves living like hell while claiming to know Jesus or to believe all the right things.

Set Free

Because it's apparently not a new thing to assume that people can be part of the kingdom of God without ever following Jesus anywhere, I wonder if it was ever as politically incorrect to speak about hell in the first century as it is today.

Yet Jesus said the truth would set us free. Always. Even inconvenient truth.[15]

For those of us who accept and live by this inconvenient and unpopular truth, the cross and salvation are returned to their rightful place at the center of the gospel. Evangelism once again becomes an important priority. And obedience once again becomes the defining mark of what it means to love God.[16]

DO DEAD PEOPLE GO TO A BETTER PLACE?

Jesus answered, "I am the way and the truth and the life. No one comes to the Father except through me."

JOHN 14:6

"Enter through the narrow gate. For wide is the gate and broad is the road that leads to destruction, and many enter through it. But small is the gate and narrow the road that leads to life, and only a few find it."

MATTHEW 7:13–14

The acts of the sinful nature are obvious: sexual immorality, impurity and debauchery; idolatry and witchcraft; hatred, discord, jealousy, fits of rage, selfish ambition, dissensions, factions and envy; drunkenness, orgies, and the like. *I warn you, as I did before, that those who live like this will not inherit the kingdom of God.*

GALATIANS 5:19–21

FINAL
THOUGHTS

It was an early summer morning when I sat down with a fresh cup of coffee and the *Los Angeles Times* to catch up on what was happening in my world. I hadn't read long when a brief article caught my eye. It reported a strange incident that had taken place in Jerusalem. It also carried a strong warning about the overuse of bug spray. But more about that later. Here's what I read.

JERUSALEM (UPI)—An Israeli woman's all-out war on a cockroach launched a series of mishaps that put her unsuspecting husband in the hospital with burns, two broken ribs, and a cracked pelvis.

The incident, reported Thursday by the Jerusalem Post, occurred last week when a woman from the Tel Aviv area, whose name was withheld, found a cockroach in her living room.

She stomped the bug and tossed it into the toilet. When the critter refused to die, she sprayed an entire can of insecticide into the toilet bowl to finish it off.

Her unsuspecting husband came home from work moments after, perched on the toilet seat and lit up a cigarette. When he finished smoking, he tossed the butt into the toilet.

The cigarette ignited the insecticide fumes and burned "his sensitive parts," the Post reported.

As they carried the man down the steps of his house, paramedics asked how he received the peculiar burns. When he responded, they laughed and accidentally dropped the stretcher, causing the man further injuries, the Post said.[1]

Hard to Believe

I laughed and showed the article to my wife. But I remember thinking that it was hard to believe something like that could really happen. Nothing in the story rang true to my own life experiences.

I had a hard time imagining someone emptying a can of bug spray in a small bathroom without gagging long before the task was finished. I couldn't fathom someone else immediately walking in and sitting down. The room would smell too bad for that. And though I'm not a smoker, I also had a hard time figuring out how the guy with the singed private parts could sit on the toilet, smoke a cigarette, and flick the ashes into the basin all at the same time—unless, of course, he was a performer with Cirque du Soleil.

But none of that really mattered. It was obviously a true story. It wasn't some myth passed along at the water cooler. Its source wasn't somebody's long-lost aunt, who just happened to know the best friend of a paramedic who once worked with one of the guys who dropped the man with the embarrassing burns.

No, this was the real deal, reported by none other than the *L.A.*

Times, the *Jerusalem Post,* and United Press International. These guys vet their stuff. They're authoritative sources that other news outlets and newscasters quote.

So I did what most of us do when we hear something that doesn't fit with our experience and makes no sense—but comes from a highly credible source. I believed it. I even passed it on as a warning to my friends who smoked. Be careful not to overuse the bug spray!

But just a couple of days later, I noticed something else. It was a tiny notice buried in the back pages with a bunch of other stuff that no one ever reads. Not sure why it caught my eye, but it did.

It was a retraction.

It seems the *L.A. Times* had been taken in by an urban legend. Not just the *L.A. Times;* also the *Jerusalem Post* and UPI.

How could that be?

How could a world-class news organization like the *L.A. Times,* with an enormous staff vetting everything that goes into the paper, be taken in by something as far-fetched as the Israeli hoax?

> *How can we protect ourselves against the myths and legends that may come our way? The answer is found in asking two basic questions: (1) How does this idea or teaching match up with the way life really works? (2) How does this idea or teaching match up with what the Bible says?*

Fact is, they got snookered by an urban legend in the same way you and I get snookered by spiritual urban legends. They believed something primarily because of the reliable source it came from—and that trumped the fact that it contradicted common sense and a lifetime of experiences. The *Jerusalem Post* believed it. UPI believed it. So the *L.A. Times* believed it—and passed it on.

We fall into the same trap in the spiritual realm when we allow our worldview and spiritual paradigms to be based on what we've always heard (or what everyone else believes) rather than careful examination that asks, "Is this really true?"

As we've seen in the unmasking of the ten spiritual urban legends contained in this book, upon closer examination they all fail the common-sense, the how-does-life-really-work, and the what-does-the-Bible-really-say test.

Yet many still believe them anyway. Like the legend of the exploding toilet, they gain their credibility because they are passed on by reputable sources: friends, Sunday-school teachers, Bible study leaders, and pastors.

Two Simple Questions

So, what's the best way to keep that from happening? How can we protect ourselves not only against these ten spiritual urban legends, but against all the myths and legends that may come our way?

The answer is found in continually asking two basic questions before believing and acting upon anything presented as a biblical principle or truth, no matter whom it comes from: (1) How does this idea or teaching match up with the way life really works? (2) How does this idea or teaching match up with what the Bible says? Not just one verse, but the entire Bible.

The genuine promises and principles of Scripture will have no problem passing through that gauntlet. The clichés, urban legends, and Sunday-school myths will inevitably fail on both accounts.

Who Moved the Line?

Yet even the right questions can't spare us if we're unwilling to accept the answers we don't want to hear.

I'm constantly amazed by the number of people I run into who decide what they will believe not so much based on the facts as on what they wish the facts were. And it's not just in the spiritual realm. You can see it in the way they approach nearly everything from science to relationships to their personal finances and even to their medical issues.

They remind me of the leaders in a village that was decimated by the massive 1999 Turkish earthquake. Apparently, thirty years before, the government had warned the village leaders that their town was situated on top of a major fault line. They were told they needed to relocate. But instead of relocating, they met in solemn assembly and decided to redraw the geological map, moving the fault line on all the regional maps so that it no longer showed their village to be in danger.[2]

Like most wishful thinking, it worked out well for a while. In fact, for nearly three decades, it brought peace and comfort to those who lived in the town. It spared everyone the hassle of moving. It kept them connected with their heritage. It sustained real estate values. And it hurt no one—that is, until the earthquake hit.

We can do the same thing spiritually. When we run into a truth we don't like, we can move the line. And the truth is, when we do, it can work out quite well—for a while.

But sooner or later, truth always shows up.

I think that's why the example of the Bereans is so important to learn from. As we saw in the opening pages of this book, they set the standard for spiritual myth busting. Even the apostle Paul was not immune from their prove-it-to-me attitude. They checked the Scriptures daily to see if what he said was so. It wasn't a lack of faith; it was a love of the truth.[3]

It's a pattern worth following. Admittedly, at times, it will put us at odds with some of the conventional wisdom and understanding of our day. But if it aligns us with Scripture and the way life really works, that's a good place to be. It does no good to move the fault line.

> "If you call out for insight and cry aloud for understanding, and if you look for it as for silver and search for it as for hidden treasure, then you will understand the fear of the LORD and find the knowledge of God. For the LORD gives wisdom, and from his mouth come knowledge and understanding. He holds victory in store for the upright, he is a shield to those whose walk is blameless, for he guards the course of the just and protects the way of his faithful ones. Then you will understand what is right and just and fair—every good path. For wisdom will enter your heart, and knowledge will be pleasant to your soul. Discretion will protect you, and understanding will guard you."
>
> PROVERBS 2:3–11

Discussion Guide

Ten Dumb Things Smart Christians Believe is a book designed to be pondered. Its head-on challenge of spiritual clichés and widely held beliefs will leave some readers feeling as if their sacred cows have been skewered. Others will feel the exhilarating confirmation that they're not the only one who has noticed that the emperor has no clothes. But no matter how it makes us feel, what matters most is how these ideas and the spiritual urban legends they question match up with Scripture.

That's why this book is best read with a pen in hand and a Bible nearby.

For many, an even better way to get the most out of it is to gather a group of friends and work through the study questions chapter by chapter. Whether you're a longtime Christian seeking new insights or a window shopper just checking out Christianity, you'll find them to be provocative and clarifying.

You'll also notice that the answers don't just come from the contents of this book. Many of the questions will drive you to Scripture for answers. The chapter-by-chapter format can easily fit into a ten-week schedule.

You'll get the most out of your study together if everyone actually writes down their answers before each meeting. That's because the first person to speak up in a group often sets a tone and direction that everyone else adjusts their answers to fit in with. But by coming with your own answers already written out, the temptation to simply piggyback on what has already been said is easily overcome. The result will be more authentic answers and much greater depth and breadth for the entire group.

By the way, don't feel that your group has to answer every question. Camp on the ones that are most helpful and stimulating, and breeze by or skip altogether the ones that don't work. This is not a test—it's a tool to spur you on to deeper study and to help you develop a worldview and lifestyle that more closely aligns with Scripture.

If you prefer a solo journey, these questions will benefit you as well. They're designed to move the concepts and principles from the idealism of the written page into the messy world of real life. They'll help you think through, reconsider, and at times resolidify your understanding of what it means to live life in the light of God's Word and truth.

Blessings on your journey,

Larry Osborne

Dumb Idea 1: Faith Can Fix Anything

John's faith and Susan's cancer ■ *Why positive thinking can't change anything* ■ *The big problem with faith in faith* ■ *How the English language mucks up everything* ■ *How faith sometimes makes things worse* ■ *One story you can bet the kids in Sunday school will never hear* ■ *The one thing faith can always fix* ■ *What a geographical moron and a GPS have in common with a life of faith*

1. What principles or insights from this chapter did you find to be...
   - most helpful?

- most challenging?
- most troubling?
- Why?

2. Prior to reading this chapter, how would you have responded to the statement, "Faith can fix anything"? Would you have agreed or disagreed? Why?

3. Have you ever been in a situation like John's where you felt you had absolute faith that God was going to step in and fix a situation, only to have him do something different?
    - If so, how did that impact your walk with God—and your ideas about faith?
    - If not, have you seen this in someone else? How did it impact their walk with God?

4. We saw that the English language tends to treat faith, belief, and trust as three completely distinct concepts, while the original Greek of the New Testament makes no such distinction. How do you think most people you know would define each of the following?
    - *faith*
    - *belief*
    - *trust*

5. Read the story of Peter's release from prison in Acts 12:1–19.
    - Write down every element of surprise or doubt you can find in the story.

- Now write down everything that shows faithful obedience despite any doubt.

6. Read Hebrews 11:29–40. How often (if ever) have you heard a sermon or study that focused on the last verses of this passage (verses 35–40)?
   - Why do you think that is so?
   - How did these verses strike you when you first read them?

Dumb Idea 2: Forgiving Means Forgetting

Four goofy ideas about forgiveness ■ *The myth of a forgetful God* ■ *The two realms of forgiveness* ■ *Are justice and forgiveness mutually exclusive?* ■ *The strange math of score keeping—why it is nearly always inaccurate* ■ *The power of a good mirror* ■ *Something for Calvinists and Arminians to fight about* ■ *The prayer of permission* ■ *Why you might want to take a sin walk—and how God will meet you there*

1. What principles or insights from this chapter did you find to be…
   - most helpful?
   - most challenging?
   - most troubling?
   - Why?

2. Prior to reading this chapter, how would you have responded to the statement, "Forgiving means forgetting"? Would you have agreed or disagreed? Why?

3. The story of Aaron's struggle with forgiving his son's murderer pointed out his faulty assumption that forgiving
meant acting as if nothing had ever happened. Have you
ever found yourself struggling to forgive because of the
same assumption—or a sense that forgiving would mean
they got away with it?

- If so, what happened? And how did it impact
  your own life?
- If not, have you seen this same response in
  someone else? How did it appear to impact
  them?

4. This chapter pointed out that the words *forget* and *remember* in the English language mostly refer to our ability to
mentally recall something, while in the Bible they mostly
refer to God ignoring or renewing his focus on someone
or something. Were you convinced? Did you buy the
argument?

- If not, why not?
- If so, how does that impact the way you should
  personally forgive others?

5. God's forgiveness doesn't always (or often) remove all the
earthly consequences. No story better illustrates this than
David's sin with Bathsheba. Read 2 Samuel 12:1–20 and
write down everything it says or implies about sin, forgiveness, and consequences. Be sure to write down not
only the obvious, but also any subtle implications you
can find.

6. At the end of this chapter, two tools were suggested as being helpful for those times when forgiveness seems out of reach (the prayer of permission and a sin walk). Sometime this week, take your own personal sin walk and then jot down your observations.
   • What did you learn about God?
   • What did you learn about yourself?
   • Is there anything you should do in response?

Dumb Idea 3: A Godly Home Guarantees Godly Kids

Why Don and Sharon hate it when their friends pull out the pictures ■ *Mike and Rhonda's head-in-the-sand optimism* ■ *The one promise lots of parents count on that isn't really a promise—and why it doesn't say what most people think it says* ■ *How B. F. Skinner snuck into our churches* ■ *Mitch's foolish pride* ■ *How Ten Rules for Raising Godly Kids became Three Suggestions for Surviving Parenthood* ■ *Why bad kids often make great adults*

1. What principles or insights from this chapter did you find to be…
   • most helpful?
   • most challenging?
   • most troubling?
   • Why?

2. Prior to reading this chapter, how would you have responded to the statement, "A godly home pretty much guarantees godly kids"? Would you have agreed or disagreed? Why?

3. Read Proverbs 1:1–6. How did you respond to the statement and observations that proverbs aren't promises? Was that a new thought or something you've seen or been taught before?

- Take a quick perusal through the book of Proverbs or a few chapters of Proverbs. Note any verses that describe the way life generally works—but for which you have personally seen a clear-cut exception.

4. Proverbs 22:6 is at the center of the storm when it comes to the myth that a godly home guarantees godly kids. Read it again. And then jot down your observations.

- Why do you think so many people assume this verse promises that a rebel will return?
- What are some of the benefits you can think of that would come from understanding this verse correctly? (Write down as many as you can think of.)

5. Read Deuteronomy 6:5–7 and Ephesians 6:4.

- What do these verses say to us about parental responsibility?
- What are some practical ways to carry out these instructions today?

6. Read the sad story of Eli's failure to restrain his sons in 1 Samuel 2:22–24, 3:11–18, 4:14–18 and then read Ezekiel 18:1–20.

- Why do you think Eli did so little to stop his sons?

- How do you reconcile Eli's lack of restraint with his sons with the statements in Ezekiel 18:1–20?

7. Just for fun. If you had to assign percentages to the things that most influence our personality and character (before and after Christ), what would you put down for each of the following and why?
    - genetics: ___%
    - environment: ___%
    - choices: ___%

Dumb Idea 4: God Has a Blueprint for My Life

Why does the search for God's will feel like an Easter egg hunt? ■ *Why a blueprint is a bad metaphor for God's will—and why a game plan is a great metaphor for God's will* ■ *Is there a reason why the New Testament ignores the kind of decisions we typically stress over?* ■ *Why God doesn't do consulting, and what happens when we think he does* ■ *How obedience makes everything (even some pretty lousy decisions) better*

1. What principles or insights from this chapter did you find to be...
    - most helpful?
    - most challenging?
    - most troubling?
    - Why?

2. Prior to reading this chapter, how would you have responded to the statement, "God has a blueprint for my life"? Would you have agreed or disagreed? Why?

3. Think back to the story of the college group asked to describe the ideal mate. How would you have responded to the assignment? How would you have responded to the question, "Why would that person want to marry you?"

   - More important, when it comes to your own life and God's will, are you currently more focused on finding or becoming?
   - What are some of the evidences?
   - What, if any, changes would help you better focus on becoming?

4. Clearly there are some times and situations when God has a blueprint for people. Here are two examples. Look up each one and then write down your observations regarding God's will.

   - Jonah 1:1–3:3
   - Hosea 1:1–3 and 3:1

5. It was pointed out in this chapter that seeing God's will as a detailed blueprint can leave us paralyzed when it comes to decision making. Have you ever found yourself paralyzed by the fear of making a wrong choice?

   - If so, what happened?
   - If not, have you seen this in someone else? What was the result?

6. The more we obey what we already know, the more of God's light we get. Read each of the following verses and write down what each passage has to say to us about God's will.

- Proverbs 4:18–19
- Ephesians 5:17–18
- Ephesians 6:5–8
- 1 Thessalonians 4:3–8
- 1 Peter 2:13–14

Dumb Idea 5: Christians Shouldn't Judge

How to get your non-Christian friends to quote the Bible ■ *Why "Do not judge" doesn't mean what most people think it means* ■ *When and how the idea of tolerance changed from "You have the right to be wrong" into "Nobody is wrong"* ■ *Log-eye disease* ■ *Did God really forget to put some important stuff in the Bible?* ■ *Why it's a bad idea to judge non-Christians by Christian standards* ■ *Are judgment and grace incompatible?*

1. What principles or insights from this chapter did you find to be…
   - most helpful?
   - most challenging?
   - most troubling?
   - Why?

2. Prior to reading this chapter, how would you have responded to the statement, "Christians shouldn't judge"? Would you have agreed or disagreed? Why?

3. The chapter notes that *tolerance* no longer means the freedom to be wrong—it now means that everyone is right.

- How has this modern redefinition impacted your life and outlook?
- Why do you think so many people believe that sincerity is all it takes to make something true in the spiritual realm?
- How have you found that to impact your own thinking and values?

4. Here are some scriptures that describe the proper way to judge. Look up each one and write down your observations.
   - Matthew 7:1–6
   - 1 Corinthians 5:9–13
   - Galatians 1:6–9
   - 2 Thessalonians 3:14–15
   - 1 John 2:3–6

5. Sometimes we can try to help God out by making judgments in areas he doesn't seem to care all that much about—or has granted freedom. Here are some passages that speak to that tendency. Write down the main point of each one.
   - Proverbs 30:5–6
   - Romans 7:15–25
   - Romans 14:1–15:7

6. The old cliché of loving the sinner but hating the sin is something we actually do quite well with ourselves. Can you think of someone you need to offer that kind of grace to?

Dumb Idea 6:
Everything Happens for a Reason

Nancy's cancer ■ *Happy talk and other stupid things people say* ■ *How Romans 8:28 became the most misunderstood and misquoted verse in the Bible* ■ *Two conditions most people don't seem to notice* ■ *Are self-inflicted wounds God's doing?* ■ *Why Murphy matters* ■ *Can a bad thing be a good thing?* ■ *Why we might want Jesus to wait a while before coming back* ■ *The power in a path called obedience*

1. What principles or insights from this chapter did you find to be...
   • most helpful?
   • most challenging?
   • most troubling?
   • Why?

2. Prior to reading this chapter, how would you have responded to the statement, "Everything happens for a reason"? Would you have agreed or disagreed? Why?

3. Have you ever been on the receiving end of well-meaning but hurtful clichés similar to those that Nancy received during her cancer?
   • If so, how did you respond?
   • If not, have you ever been the one passing on happy talk in an attempt to be helpful?
   • How did people respond?

4. In this chapter we saw that Romans 8:28 has some conditions that are often overlooked. What do the following verses have to say about these conditions?
    a. "who love him"
       • John 14:15
    b. "who have been called according to his purpose"
       • Romans 1:5–7
       • 1 Timothy 6:12
       • 2 Timothy 2:10

5. Here are two verses that speak to our tendency to claim that something bad was actually good because of the good God brought out of it. Read each one and jot down your thoughts.
    • Genesis 50:20
    • Isaiah 5:20

6. When it comes to most of the bad stuff that happens in your life and the lives of those you know, what percentage would you assign to each of the following categories—and why?
    • the self-inflicted wounds of sin: ___%
    • the self-inflicted wounds of a foolish decision: ___%
    • the unavoidable backwash of living in a fallen world: ___%
    • God's Plan A: ___%

Dumb Idea 7: Let Your Conscience Be Your Guide

The one type of person I've never been able to help ■ *The musings of a tax dodger* ■ *A Jiminy Cricket code of ethics—why so many people trust it and why that's not a smart thing to do* ■ *How our conscience is more like a thermostat than a thermometer* ■ *Blind spots and bad software* ■ *What heart disease does to our conscience* ■ *The one thing everyone's conscience does with unerring accuracy*

1. What principles or insights from this chapter did you find to be...
   - most helpful?
   - most challenging?
   - most troubling?
   - Why?

2. Prior to reading this chapter, how would you have responded to the statement, "It's a good idea to let your conscience be your guide"? Would you have agreed or disagreed? Why?

3. Have you ever dealt with someone whose foolish or sinful choices messed up their life but they still refused to take responsibility because they were following their consciences? If so, what happened?

4. Have you ever followed your conscience to a really bad decision?
   - If so, what happened?
   - What did you learn from the experience?

5. This chapter pointed out that our conscience is more like a thermostat that we set to our comfort zone than a thermometer that gives us an accurate reading of the facts.

    - Can you think of a time when you reset or recalibrated your conscience so that what once seemed wrong felt right, or vice versa?
    - What led to the change?
    - Can you think of a previous spiritual blind spot that you now see clearly?

6. Read 1 Corinthians 4:4. How does it strike you that an apostle would feel this way about his conscience?

7. Read Romans 12:2 and 2 Timothy 3:16–17.
    - What are you currently doing to be sure your conscience is properly calibrated?
    - Is there anything you should start or stop doing to better align your conscience with God's heart and values?

Dumb Idea 8: God Brings Good Luck

Why I worry when someone angles to be last in line ■ *Tim's rather "unusual" choice of words* ■ *The high price of unrealistic and unfounded promises* ■ *Job's wife and Asaph's journal* ■ *Eddie Haskell Christians—do they really think God is stupid?* ■ *Do we?* ■ *Why it's never a good idea to judge a king's banquet by the finger food* ■ *One cliché that's not only wrong but flat-out absurd* ■ *Why an abundant life might not be so abundant*

1. What principles or insights from this chapter did you find to be…
   - most helpful?
   - most challenging?
   - most troubling?
   - Why?

2. Prior to reading this chapter, how would you have responded to the statement, "Following God brings good luck"? Would you have agreed or disagreed? Why?

3. This chapter tells the story of Tim's tirade. Have you ever known someone who turned on God because life didn't work out as they thought?
   - If so, what happened?
   - Is there anything you can learn from observing their experience?

4. Read Psalm 73. Have you ever felt the same kind of confusion Asaph felt?
   - If so, what caused it?
   - Did anything happen to put things in proper perspective?

5. Eddie Haskell Christians seem to think that God is stupid or at least can't see what we do outside of church. Where have you seen examples of Eddie Haskell Christianity or empty cultural Christianity?
   - What has been the impact on those people?

- What has been the impact on non-Christians who were watching?

6. Here are some passages that suggest following God doesn't always bring such good luck. Read each one and jot down your observations.
    - Job 1–2
    - Proverbs 11:8
    - Proverbs 24:15–16
    - Mark 13:13
    - Luke 9:22–23
    - Ephesians 1:17–21

Dumb Idea 9: A Valley Means a Wrong Turn

Why my Dark Years had nothing to do with a wrong turn ■ *How extended valleys can make our friends' advice nearly worthless* ■ *Three simple but profound fog-cutting questions* ■ *The kind of valley we never want to leave prematurely* ■ *Shortcuts we don't want to take, even if they work* ■ *The day a bunch of guys with iron chariots proved to be stronger than a bunch of guys with God on their side* ■ *What to do when God says, "Get someone else to help you"*

1. What principles or insights from this chapter did you find to be…
    - most helpful?
    - most challenging?
    - most troubling?
    - Why?

2. Prior to reading this chapter, how would you have responded to the statement, "A valley usually means a wrong turn"? Would you have agreed or disagreed? Why?

3. Have you ever found yourself in a valley that you knew was a *God sent me here* valley?
   • If so, how did you know it was a *God sent me here* valley?
   • How did you respond when things got tough?
   • What did you learn?

4. Read Exodus 14:1–31. Write down every insight you can find in this passage about *God sent me here* valleys.

5. Read 2 Samuel 11:1–12:20 and Proverbs 19:3. Then write down any insights you find in these passages about *I messed up* valleys.

6. Read Judges 10:10–16.
   • Does God's response in this passage surprise you?
   • Can you think of a time when you've seen God respond this way in your life or the life of a friend? If so, what happened?

Dumb Idea 10: Dead People Go to a Better Place

How to start a mini riot ■ *The truth about wicked Uncle Ernie* ■ *Funeral assurances and the frantic search for a nod-to-God* ■ *Blame Jesus* ■ *The myth behind the myth* ■ *A rather testy e-mail* ■ *How and when did obedience become an extra-credit assignment?* ■ *Why Mickey Cohen couldn't be a Christian gangster* ■ *The big difference between struggling and setting up camp* ■ *The one telltale sign of whether or not we love God*

1. What principles or insights from this chapter did you find to be…
   - most helpful?
   - most challenging?
   - most troubling?
   - Why?

2. Prior to reading this chapter, how would you have responded to the statement, "Most people end up in heaven"? Would you have agreed or disagreed? Why?

3. Can you think of a time when you heard someone offer funeral assurances even though the person who died clearly wanted nothing to do with following God?

4. There's no question that the idea that Jesus is the only way to heaven has become politically incorrect, even among some Christians. Here are some passages that speak to the issue. Look up each one and rewrite it in your own words using modern-day language.
   - Matthew 7:13–14
   - Matthew 10:28
   - Mark 8:36
   - John 14:6
   - Galatians 2:21

5. This chapter pointed out that when it's assumed that
   most people go to heaven anyway, it has a negative impact
   upon evangelism. Which of the following impacts do you
   think is most common among the Christians you know
   (and why)?
   - A loss of urgency (They'll go to heaven anyway.)
   - A fear of coming off as arrogant (Who are we to
     say Jesus is the only way?)
   - A secondary priority (Physical and justice needs
     come first.)

6. Read the story of the rich young ruler in Matthew
   19:16–30.
   - How do you think most Christians you know
     would respond if someone came up with the same
     request today?
   - Why?
   - What would you tell the person—and why?

7. What, if any, impact do you think the following verses
   should have upon the way we share the gospel?
   - Proverbs 31:8–9
   - Micah 6:8
   - 1 John 3:17–20

Acknowledgments

I want to extend special thanks to:

The amazing congregation at North Coast Church, thank you for the privilege of serving as your pastor these many years. You have taught me much. I hope I've returned the favor in a small way.

Many of the life lessons and stories in these pages find their genesis in our shared spiritual journey. Of course, where appropriate, I've taken the liberty to change names, minor details, and just enough of our story to retain its essence without letting everyone else figure out who the players were. But my bet is that many of you will recognize yourself and hopefully smile as you remember the valley we walked through together or the mountaintop we climbed.

I often tell people that I wish everyone could have the privilege of sitting on my side of the desk for just a season. It's a place where I've seen and experienced firsthand the best and the worst of Christianity. It's a place where both heartache and victories are shared— often within minutes of each other. It's a place where masks are removed, secrets revealed, images set aside, and hard truths shared. There's no way to sit on this side of the desk and not be changed. It's the ultimate cliché killer.

David Kopp, thanks for your encouraging belief in this project and your invaluable guidance. I appreciate your willingness to let me keep my voice and heart and for not insisting that I take the "safe" path when the risky one was closer to the truth.

Bucky Rosenbaum, let me express my gratitude for your invaluable wisdom and experience in helping me understand the nuances of publishing that are far beyond my expertise and experience.

Erica Ramos and Kathie Duncan, thanks for your careful proofing and honest feedback. You both helped make the clear parts of this book clearer. As for the fuzzy stuff, we all know that some parts were beyond repair.

My colleagues in ministry, especially Charlie Bradshaw, Paul Savona, and Chris Brown, thanks for making nearly every day I go in to work a good day and for allowing me to appear a lot wiser than I am when I take the things we've learned together and pass them off as my own.

My folks, Bill and Carolyn Osborne, I rise up and call you blessed for living out your faith without the slightest bit of pretense or hypocrisy. You made it easy for Bob, Linda, and me to know and love God. Thanks for never being afraid when we questioned the status quo and for actually encouraging us to do so. It's served each of us well in our chosen professions and walks with God.

Nancy, thanks for being my best friend and my most honest critic. You always help me hone my thoughts and never let me get away with sloppy thinking or lazy writing. I married up, big time.

Finally, Nathan (and Marie), Rachel, and Josh, thank you for sharing Dad with the wider body of Christ. You are my ministry that matters most. You are the ministry I'm most proud of. Your character, integrity, and love for God make me a very blessed man.

Notes

Introduction: Spiritual Urban Legends
1. See Acts 17:11.
2. See 1 Corinthians 3:18–19.

Dumb Idea 1: Faith Can Fix Anything
1. See Hebrews 11:1.
2. See John 3:16; 1 John 2:3–5; James 2:19–22.
3. The synonymous nature of faith, belief, and trust can be seen in Hebrews 11:1 ("Faith is being sure of what we hope for"), John 3:16 ("Whoever believes in him shall not perish"), and John 14:1 ("Trust in God; trust also in me"). In these three passages the words *faith, belief,* and *trust* are all differing forms of the same word. (The only difference is that Hebrews 11:1 uses it as a noun, while John 3:16 and 14:1 use it as a verb.)
4. See James 2:19–26.
5. See Acts 12:1–16. See also Larry Osborne, *Spirituality for the Rest of Us: A Down-to-Earth Guide to Knowing God* (Colorado Springs, CO: Multnomah, 2009). This book was originally published as *A Contrarian's Guide to Knowing God.*
6. Hebrews 11:39.
7. Hebrews 11:6.
8. See John 3:16; Romans 1:5; 5:1; James 2:21–23; 1 Peter 1:9; 1 John 2:3–5.

Dumb Idea 2: Forgiving Means Forgetting

1. See Jeremiah 31:34; Hebrews 8:12.
2. See Psalm 103:11–12; Micah 7:19.
3. See Genesis 7:23–8:1.
4. See Matthew 6:9–15; 18:21–35; Luke 6:37.
5. See 2 Samuel 12:1–20.
6. See Mathew 18:21–22; Luke 17:3–5.
7. Matthew 18:35.
8. See Matthew 6:12; Colossians 3:13.
9. Luke 23:34.
10. See Matthew 12:22–32.
11. See Matthew 5:39; Luke 17:3.
12. See Romans 12:17–21.
13. 2 Timothy 4:14; 1 Timothy 1:20.
14. Romans 12:19.
15. See Proverbs 14:15.
16. For more on this, see Larry Osborne, *Spirituality for the Rest of Us: A Down-to-Earth Guide to Knowing God* (Colorado Springs, CO: Multnomah, 2009).

Dumb Idea 3: A Godly Home Guarantees Godly Kids

1. See Deuteronomy 6:5–7; Ephesians 6:4; Colossians 3:21.
2. See Luke 15:11–32.
3. See Psalm 51:5; Ezekiel 18:1–20; Jeremiah 17:9; Romans 5:12.
4. See Proverbs 21:30–31.
5. See Genesis 2:17; 3:1–19.
6. See 1 Samuel 2:22–24; 3:11–18; 4:14–18; Romans 15:4; 1 Corinthians 10:11.
7. See 1 Timothy 3:1–5; Titus 1:6.

8. See 1 Timothy 3:6.

9. See Jeremiah 9:23–24; 2 Corinthians 10:17.

Dumb Idea 4: God Has a Blueprint for My Life

1. See Jonah 1:1–3:3.

2. See Deuteronomy 1:32–33; Jeremiah 18:1–6; Acts 16:6–10.

3. See 1 Corinthians 6:15–20; 1 Thessalonians 4:3–8.

4. Matthew 11:28–30.

5. See Proverbs 4:18–19; Romans 1:21–32. See also Larry Osborne, *Spirituality for the Rest of Us: A Down-to-Earth Guide to Knowing God* (Colorado Springs, CO: Multnomah, 2009).

6. See Proverbs 1:24–32; 28:9.

7. See Proverbs 19:2–3; 22:3.

8. See Acts 17:11.

9. See Deuteronomy 13:1–4; 18:18–22.

10. Abraham's story is found in Genesis 12–25.

11. See Hebrews 11:19.

12. See Romans 12:2.

13. See 1 Timothy 2:3–4; 2 Peter 3:9.

14. See Ephesians 5:18; 6:5–8; 1 Thessalonians 4:3–8; 1 Peter 2:13–15.

Dumb Idea 5: Christians Shouldn't Judge

1. See Matthew 7:6, NKJV.

2. See Matthew 7:15–20.

3. See Matthew 7:6–16; 1 Corinthians 5:9–13; Galatians 1:8–9; 2 Thessalonians 3:14–15; 1 John 2:3–5. These are just a few of many passages giving us standards to judge by.

4. See John 8:1–11.

5. John 8:11.

6. See Matthew 7:2; Romans 2:1.

7. See Matthew 7:1–2.

8. See Matthew 7:3–5.

9. See Romans 7:15–25.

10. See 1 Corinthians 6:18–20.

11. See Proverbs 30:5–6; Romans 14:1–15:7.

12. See 1 Corinthians 11:19.

13. See John 14:6.

14. See 1 Corinthians 5:9–13.

15. See Matthew 7:15–27; Galatians 1:6–9; 1 John 4:1–3.

16. See 1 Corinthians 5:1–13; Galatians 6:1; 2 Thessalonians 3:13–15.

17. See 2 Timothy 2:23–26.

18. See Matthew 22:36–40.

Dumb Idea 6: Everything Happens for a Reason

1. See Romans 12:15.

2. See Genesis 3:12.

3. See John 14:15; Romans 1:6–7; 2 Thessalonians 2:14; 1 Timothy 6:12; 2 Timothy 2:10.

4. See Genesis 3; Romans 5:12; 8:19–22.

5. See 2 Timothy 2:12–13; 1 Peter 4:12–13.

6. See Proverbs 19:2–3.

7. See Proverbs 22:3.

8. See Proverbs 19:3.

9. Genesis 50:20.

10. See 2 Corinthians 4:4.

11. See 2 Peter 3:3–10.

12. See Hebrews 13:5.

Dumb Idea 7: Let Your Conscience Be Your Guide

1. See Matthew 17:24–27; Romans 13:1–7.
2. See Romans 7:14–25.
3. See Acts 15:36–40; 16:6–10; 2 Corinthians 1:8; 12:7–9.
4. See Psalm 119:9–11; Romans 12:1–2; 2 Timothy 3:16–17.

Dumb Idea 8: God Brings Good Luck

1. See Deuteronomy 28:1–68; Proverbs 3:33; 10:24–25; 11:8; 24:15–16.
2. See Job 2:9–10; 4–5.
3. Psalm 73:13–14.
4. See Job 2:9–10; Psalm 73:16–24.
5. See Genesis 4:3–9.
6. See Matthew 5:11–12; 16:24–25; 19:29; Luke 14:26–35; John 15:18; 15:20.
7. See Job 2:10.
8. See 2 Chronicles 36:5–21.
9. See Revelation 3:15–16.
10. See 1 Corinthians 15:13–19.
11. See Matthew 5:10–12; Mark 13:13; Luke 9:23–26; 14:26.
12. See Romans 5:1–6; 14:17; 15:13; Ephesians 1:17–21.
13. See 1 Timothy 6:5–6.

Dumb Idea 9: A Valley Means a Wrong Turn

1. See Larry Osborne, *The Unity Factor: Developing a Healthy Church Leadership Team*, 4th ed. (Vista, CA: Owl's Nest, 2006); and Larry Osborne, *Sticky Church* (Grand Rapids, MI: Zondervan, 2008).
2. See Deuteronomy 28:14–68; Proverbs 19:3; Matthew 7:24–27.

3. See Hebrews 11:1–12:3; James 1:2–4.

4. See Psalm 15:1–5.

5. See Genesis 15:12–14; 47:1–12; Exodus 1:5–14.

6. See Exodus 14.

7. See Matthew 3:13–4:11.

8. See Luke 8:22–26.

9. See 2 Samuel 11:1–12:15.

10. See Job 1–2.

11. See Judges 1:19.

12. See Genesis 12:10–20; 20:1–7; 26:6–11; 27:15–20; the book of Jonah.

13. See Daniel 6.

14. See Judges 10:10–14.

15. Judges 10:15.

16. See Judges 10:16.

17. See 1 Corinthians 10:13.

18. See Hebrews 11:32–40.

19. See James 1:2–5.

20. See Hebrews 5:8.

Dumb Idea 10: Dead People Go to a Better Place

1. See Matthew 18:9; Galatians 5:19–21; 2 Thessalonians 1:6–9; Revelation 20:10–15.

2. See Matthew 7:13–14.

3. See Matthew 10:2–4; 12:1–8; Luke 7:36–50; John 4:5–27.

4. See Matthew 10:28; 23:15; John 14:6; Acts 4:12.

5. See Matthew 28:18–20.

6. See Proverbs 14:31; 29:7; Micah 6:8.

7. Mark 8:36.

8. See Galatians 2:20–21.

9. See Matthew 19:16–23.

10. Charles Colson, *Loving God* (Grand Rapids, MI: Zondervan, 1983), 92.

11. See Luke 15:11–32.

12. See Romans 7:14–25.

13. 1 John 2:4.

14. See 1 Corinthians 6:9–11; Galatians 5:19–21; 6:7–9.

15. See John 8:31–32.

16. See John 14:15; 15:10.

Epilogue: Final Thoughts

1. "Israel Husband's Lament: Next Time, Dear, Why Not Just Flush the Toilet?" *Los Angeles Times,* 26 August 1988, 6.

2. Quoted by Jennifer Ludden, *All Things Considered,* National Public Radio, August 26, 1999.

3. See Acts 17:11.

About the Author

LARRY OSBORNE is a senior pastor at North Coast Church in Vista, California. His passion for a biblical Christianity that moves beyond hackneyed clichés and empty traditions has helped North Coast Church grow from a tiny congregation meeting in a rented cafeteria to more than seven thousand in weekend attendance.

Larry and North Coast have been recognized and honored as one of the most innovative and influential pastors and churches in America in numerous national surveys. Each weekend at North Coast, you'll find more than twenty different worship options on multiple nearby campuses, each targeted at a specific demographic audience. On any given weekend you're likely to find a worship venue filled with tatted up and pierced young people alongside a worship service filled with gray-haired traditionalists enjoying the great hymns of the faith—all studying the same passage and listening to the same biblical message.

It's all part of a deep commitment to presenting hard-hitting biblical truth in a way that reaches out to the many mind-sets and subcultures of our day without changing or compromising the message.

Larry is also the founder of the North Coast Training Network, a ministry that offers training and consulting to pastors and churches around the country. In addition, he writes and speaks extensively on issues related to spiritual formation and leadership. His books include *The Unity Factor: Developing a Healthy Church Leadership Team*, *Sticky Church*, and *Spirituality for the Rest of Us*. He and his wife, Nancy, live in Oceanside, California.

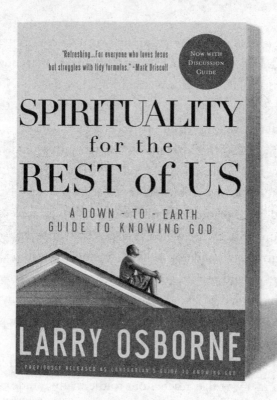

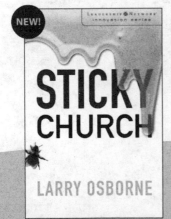